With the Compliments

of the

MINISTER FOR EDUCATION

SINGAPORE

TO

    THE SECRETARY OF EDUCATION

    UNITED STATES OF AMERICA

APEC EDUCATION MINISTERIAL MEETING

WASHINGTON DC 5 - 6 AUGUST 1992

Singapore: The Next Lap

Typeset by Superskill Graphics Pte Ltd
Colour separated by United Graphic Pte Ltd
and Magenta Lithographic Consultants
Printed by Star Standard Industries (Pte) Ltd

ISBN 981 204 253 9

"Singapore can do well only if her good sons and daughters are prepared to dedicate themselves to help others.

I shall rally them to serve the country.

For if they do not come forward, what future will we have?

I therefore call on my fellow citizens to join me, to run the next lap together."

THE NEXT LAP

singapore
singapore
singapore
singapore
singapore
singapore
singapore

Contents

Foreword
Beyond 1999

This book represents the hopes of a new generation of Singaporeans and their leaders.

It builds upon the ideas of very many Singaporeans. For several years, in private and public discussions, various government and private groups have been working on ideas for Singapore's long-term national development. In 1984 the government put forward Vision 1999. In 1986 the Economic Committee charted new strategies for economic development. 1988 saw the Agenda for Action. In 1989 six Advisory Councils deliberated on issues concerning the disabled, the aged, sports and recreation, youth, culture and the arts, and family and community life. This year we decided on our Shared Values.

In 1989, I also asked a Committee of Ministers of State to draw on the ideas that have been thrown up and present a comprehensive synthesis of our hopes and plans for Singapore over the next generation. The result is this book.

The chapters which follow cover a wide area – the life of our people, investing in the next generation, earning a good living for ourselves, making Singapore more pleasant to live in, and developing the arts and sports. Some ideas are almost ready to be implemented, others will take longer. A few need further study and elaboration. Together, they outline a programme to make Singapore more prosperous, gracious and interesting over the next 20 to 30 years.

To succeed, this programme needs the support of all Singaporeans. The government alone cannot make Singapore prosper, or make the schools and universities lively and exciting. Success depends on every Singaporean putting in his best, and building together what none of us can accomplish separately.

We may try to look many years ahead into the next century, but we cannot predict the future. History is full of surprises. We have good reasons to be optimistic, but we must not be complacent. The programme is an ambitious target, not a rosy forecast. We must work hard to turn our ideas into reality.

This book suggests ways to capitalize on the physical and social assets that an earlier generation of Singaporeans has built up over the last 25 years and improve them to match our new needs and aspirations. It represents both change and continuity.

The world is changing rapidly, but the basics remain the same. We have to make a living. Our most precious asset will always be our people. We must look after one another and build up our national spirit. Our security depends on our own efforts. Provided we are united and we anticipate our problems with ready solutions, whatever the future brings, we will be ready.

Goh Chok Tong
Prime Minister

In Brief

On November 28, 1990, a new chapter opened in Singapore's modern history. Mr Lee Kuan Yew handed the torch of leadership to Mr Goh Chok Tong. We can look back with pride and satisfaction at what Mr Lee Kuan Yew and his generation of leaders have achieved for Singapore. They have given us the second highest standard of living in Asia. We must now look beyond into the next century and prepare the conditions for our continued prosperity and security.

We need both continuity and change. Sound economic policies, hard work and good government supported by an able Civil Service have made possible our rapid social and economic development. We have become a middle-income society. We now have a good foundation for future progress.

We live in a world that is ever-changing. External events can shake us, as they have in the past. Nothing is certain. We have to keep trying to stay ahead in the race of nations. We must never forget the basics: we have to stay united, work hard, save, look after each other, be quick to seize opportunities and be vigilant to internal and external threats to our national security. No one owes us a living – we have to earn it.

People are, and will always be, our most precious resource. We must monitor closely our population structure. Within limits, our population can grow larger to support a more diversified economy. To moderate the effects of population ageing and fertility decline, we must encourage parents to have three children, and more if they can afford it. Marriage and parenthood should be valued by Singaporeans as important goals.

Singapore is what it is today because we have been able to attract talent from all over the world to work and live here. We must attract more world talent, especially Asian talent. Our city can accommodate them, and we will be the richer for it.

At the same time we must invest even more in our people and give them a stake in the common prosperity. Education will receive the highest emphasis as it is resourcefulness, not resources, that will increasingly determine winners and losers in the future. We will increase variety in education, widen parental choice and help equalize opportunities for

every generation. Every Singaporean should have at least 10 years of education. The new Edusave scheme will give each child a better chance to develop his potential to the fullest.

All our plans depend on strong economic growth. Singaporeans will have to work hard, work smart, and work together. We should not allow the physical limits of our city-state and our small population to constrain us. Our objective is to make Singapore one of the major hub cities of the world. We will keep on upgrading our infrastructure. We must also encourage more of our companies to venture overseas and think in terms of Singapore International. The Growth Triangle of Johor, Riau and Singapore will benefit Singapore and the region.

In Singapore, we live in an urban environment. We want a city that is pleasant to work and live in, a city of beauty, character and grace. To achieve this, we need variety in our physical landscape. In our master plan, green spaces, the hills, the sea, beaches and rivers are carefully woven into the urban landscape. It is a city we will be proud to call home.

Now that we have achieved a measure of affluence, we can better address the other dimension of arts and sports. We want to be a flourishing hub for culture and the arts, with both local and international participation. To keep our people fit, we will need better facilities for sports. Our objective is to be both a cultured and a rugged society.

In pursuing excellence, we should not forget the less fortunate in our midst. Our guiding principle is to help them stand on their own feet with dignity and pride, with many hands helping. The government will play its part, but we must avoid the pitfalls of a welfare state.

We live in an interdependent world. To compete effectively, we have to be international in our outlook. To help us forge our international links, we will establish the Singapore International Foundation. It will provide mechanisms for international exchange and help link Singaporeans who are overseas with one another and with the home country. We will always be good world citizens. Within our means, we will continue to provide

technical assistance to less developed countries. We will play our part, however small, to make this a better world.

With the best intentions and the best plans, we can yet fail if we do not preserve the security of our nation. We must be vigilant and always ready to defend ourselves. So long as we stay united and organized, we will be able to weather the most difficult storms.

This book sets out the broad directions for our long-term national development. Many Singaporeans have contributed ideas. Many recommendations have been made. They will be implemented progressively. Together, we will run the next lap.

People
Our Most Precious Resource

Our children, our future, our hope.

People are, and will always be, our most precious resource. More than anything else, it is the effort of Singaporeans, with their drive and talent, that has made the country what it is today. Overcoming great odds as a newly-independent nation without natural resources, we have turned our city-state into a thriving and modern economy.

The future will be no different. In the next lap, the size of our population and the quality of our people will determine how successfully we fare. We must have enough capable and talented people to do the job – and to do it well. This is crucial. Because Singapore depends so critically on its people, any change in the size of the population or its make-up will have a significant impact on the country's future.

The population is not growing fast enough to replace itself in the long term; many Singaporeans remain unmarried; and those who do marry tend to have fewer children. As a result, the population may peak in the year 2020 and thereafter begin to decline. Fortunately we have spotted the problem in time.

Too small a population will hinder our development. It will impose limits on what we can do. We will be unable to undertake certain activities for lack of capable people. Our local cultural and entertainment scene may be less exciting than elsewhere for lack of audience and talent. Our security will be less assured because there will be fewer able-bodied Singaporeans to man our armed forces.

We need not accept such constraints. We can, and we must, make sure our population grows sufficiently. We should also supplement our numbers with talent from abroad.

How successfully we do this will determine the kind of Singapore we will be in the next century. We must therefore address these problems today. We need to know how many people Singapore can accommodate comfortably, and find ways to raise the quality of the population.

"We must have enough capable and talented people to do the job – and to do it well."

Children. Life would be empty without them.

How We Got to the Present Levels

Singapore's population grew rapidly in the early years as a result of immigration from China, India and Peninsular Malaysia. In addition, these early settlers tended to have large families.

The rapidly rising population, however, posed a serious problem in the 1960s. The worry then was that too large a population would impose unbearable strains on Singapore's fledgling economy. The economic uncertainties caused by Indonesian Confrontation, separation from Malaysia and the British military withdrawal added to these fears. Hence, the government adopted a "stop-at-two" population policy. But we went below two and are now not replacing ourselves.

If we do nothing, the population will age rapidly, and in time, will start to shrink. Fewer workers will enter the job market each year, and the talent pool will decrease.

We share these problems with many developed countries. Young adults today put their careers, leisure and personal interests above marriage and parenthood. So a sizable number of Singaporeans remain unmarried.

The New Population Policy introduced in 1987 has halted the fertility decline. The fertility rate rebounded from a historic low of 1.4 in 1986 to 2.0 in 1988. But this is not good enough. For the population to replace itself, we need a rate of 2.1. That it did not reach this level even in the "Dragon" year of 1988, when a convergence of factors made it possibly the best year for mothers to have babies, is cause for concern.

We must, therefore, make a greater effort to encourage more Singaporeans to marry, to do so earlier and to have three children, and more if they can afford it.

If we do not succeed, we will face the following demographic consequences:

- If future fertility rates fall between 1.8 and 2.1, Singapore's population will start declining by the year 2020, after peaking at about 3.2 to 3.4 million.

"We must encourage more Singaporeans to marry, to do so earlier and to have three children, and more if they can afford it."

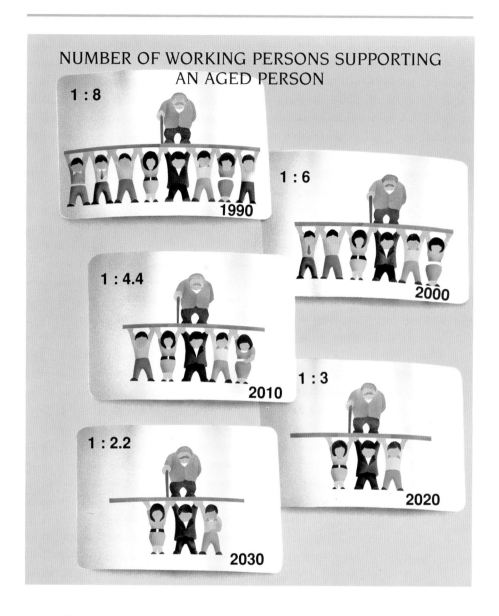

NUMBER OF WORKING PERSONS SUPPORTING
AN AGED PERSON

1 : 8
1990

1 : 6
2000

1 : 4.4
2010

1 : 3
2020

1 : 2.2
2030

- The number of elderly people will increase significantly as the post-war baby boomers reach old age. About a quarter of the population will be aged 60 and older by the year 2030 compared to 9 per cent today.

Why a Larger Population is Better

A sufficiently large population will provide many more opportunities for Singapore to grow and develop. It will provide the critical mass of talented people needed for our future development. Without enough middle and

Our children will grow into confident young adults.

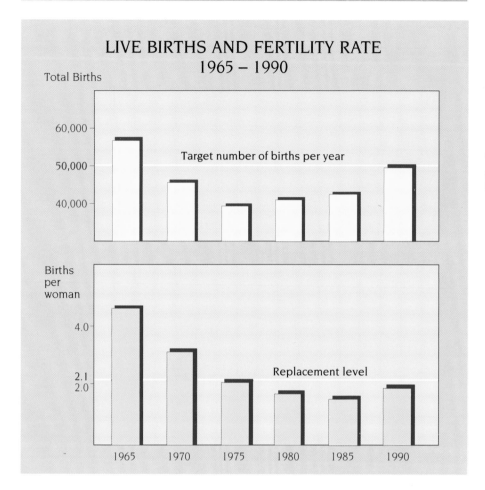

LIVE BIRTHS AND FERTILITY RATE
1965 – 1990

Total Births

60,000

Target number of births per year

50,000

40,000

Births per woman

4.0

2.1
2.0

Replacement level

1965   1970   1975   1980   1985   1990

"...we need 50,000 babies a year."

top managers, for example, many Singapore companies will not be able to go international and compete in the world market.

Having more talented and creative people will also give a boost to art and culture in Singapore.

Finally, a growing population will age more slowly. The elderly will form a smaller proportion of the population and be less of a burden on the economy.

Can Singapore accommodate a larger population? Studies have concluded that, with careful use of land, we can comfortably house 4 million people, 50 per cent more than now, and still improve our quality of life.

"...we can comfortably house 4 million people, 50 per cent more than now, and still improve our quality of life."

Wedding belles with their beaux.

Getting There

There are two ways to increase Singapore's population.

Increasing our Population Growth Rate. First, we need to increase our natural population growth rate. Broadly speaking, we need 50,000 babies a year. This means encouraging singles to marry, to start their families earlier and to have more children if they can afford to do so. We have to do this sensitively because such decisions are highly personal.

Attracting Talent. Second, we have to increase our efforts to bring talented people, especially Asians, into Singapore. Singapore's population is unlikely to increase sufficiently through indigenous growth alone, unless fertility rates increase dramatically. Our country is what it is today because we have been able to attract talent from Asia and all over the world to work and live here. This has been our heritage.

No city which draws only on indigenous talent can maintain its excellence. London draws from the whole United Kingdom; New York from the whole world.

Our economy has benefited greatly from the contributions of skilled foreign workers.

Singapore has benefited tremendously from the talent we have been able to attract. Skilled workers from abroad help run our factories and businesses. Many of our best institutions, including the Institute of Systems Science and the Institute of Molecular and Cell Biology, have thrived because local talent has been supplemented by foreign expertise. Without their contributions, our progress would have been slower.

Singapore will continue to attract talent from abroad. Our doors are open to anyone with talent or skills, and who can fit into our way of life. As talent is highly mobile, we should capitalize on our advantage as a cosmopolitan Asian city to attract Asian talent in large numbers. We are an Asian society in which they can feel at home. More talent from outside will create more opportunities for Singaporeans. We will all benefit.

"…we should capitalize on our advantage as a cosmopolitan Asian city to attract Asian talent in large numbers."

Minimizing the Outflow

Living in an open society, Singaporeans are free to stay or leave. Singaporeans generally have little difficulty adapting to life in developed countries. But we must minimize this outflow. We have to make Singapore not just a pleasant place to work and live in, but also a home.

We will find ways to give Singaporeans a greater stake in this country. Emotively, we must strengthen our national identity and national consciousness. To progress in this uncertain world, we must stand united as one people and one nation.

More recreational facilities will be built.

"We will find ways to give Singaporeans a greater stake in this country. Emotively, we must strengthen our national identity and national consciousness."

Developing our Full Potential

As a nation, we should try to develop our potential to the full, using our resources to maximum advantage.

This means developing our people – our most precious resource – to the fullest. We can afford to invest heavily in our people and we will do so. Now that we know we can house 4 million Singaporeans comfortably, we will make greater efforts to attract more talent from abroad. We should not settle for anything less.

Growing up together as Singaporeans: childhood is a carefree period in our life.

Education
Investing In Our People

As Asians, we believe that education is the key to a better life. Through education, we become more skilled, more productive and more resourceful. Education is investment in our people. Measured in terms of our national budget, our investment in education is second only to defence. The investment is paying off. We now enjoy the second highest standard of living in Asia. In the years ahead, we will invest even more in education to stay competitive and to attain higher living standards.

The school assembly (opposite) is a familiar sight every morning all over Singapore. While grooming our youth to be morally upright citizens, our education system will also develop their creative and artistic talents (above).

Our People

Our task in the years ahead is to raise the educational base of our people. Every young Singaporean will have the opportunity to enjoy at least 10 years of good basic education. Most will go on to junior colleges, polytechnics or vocational institutes, which will prepare them for their chosen careers.

We will also provide opportunities for upgrading and continuing education. Our aim is to maximize the full potential of each and every one through both formal and continuing education.

Greater Commitment to Education

We will invest more resources in education so that we will have higher quality, greater diversity and better choices.

We will raise the quality of education in Singapore. There are now places in schools, polytechnics and universities for every student who qualifies for one. The general quality of education in Singapore is good. We now have the resources to raise quality further, to make it not only good, but excellent.

While we continue to cater for the educational needs of the majority, we will also provide for those with exceptional talents, such as in art, music or languages, and for those with special learning disabilities. We will encourage greater flexibility in the running of schools and a greater diversity of programmes, so that there will be innovation and progress.

"There are now places in schools, polytechnics and universities for every student who qualifies for one."

Young children today –
Singapore's future...
Pre-school education helps to
develop our young children.

Parents play an essential role in the education of their children. They will be given more choice in how they want their children educated and in what enrichment activities their children should participate.

A Good Start for Pre-Schoolers. We will give attention to pre-school education. We will monitor and conduct research in this area.

Pre-schools and kindergartens are not a formal part of the school system, but they enjoy a large enrolment as parents see the value of pre-school education. We must make sure that these programmes cater to the developmental needs of our pre-schoolers. Parents too should be sensitized to the risks of imposing formal "hothouse" education prematurely on young children.

We will make available two routes for pre-school education. We will expand the preparatory year programme to include more primary schools. This will emphasize the learning of the mother tongue and English and the inculcation of values.

"We will give attention to pre-school education... monitor and conduct research in this area."

At the same time, we will help private kindergartens to offer two-year programmes for 4- and 5-year-olds, using the preparatory year curriculum. We will assign trained pre-school teachers to supervise and coordinate their classes.

These provisions will give parents more options for pre-school education.

Our Schools

Better Buildings, Better Facilities. At the primary and secondary levels, we will invest more in infrastructure. By 1995, 50 per cent of secondary schools will be single-session. We will build more schools so that eventually all schools, secondary and primary, can go single-session. Each school will also enjoy new and upgraded facilities.

"School of the Future" is the title of this mural conceived by Siglap Secondary students.

Single-Session Schools. Our single-session schools will have ample facilities to cater for a wide range of pupils' needs and interests. There will be flexibility for more remedial and enrichment programmes and for all-week extracurricular activity.

Pupils will participate in a broad range of programmes. They will gain from greater interaction with their peers across the levels. From these "home" classrooms and school fields will emerge a strong sense of camaraderie and belonging. The enriching and reassuring environment will nurture and stimulate young minds.

For the elementary years, we will set up day primary schools. There, pupils will learn at a better pace and be cared for while their parents are at work.

"The enriching and reassuring environment will nurture and stimulate young minds."

With smaller classes, each child will get more attention from the teacher. There will be more interaction between teacher and pupil and among pupils.

Single-session schools allow
more flexible timetables and
more opportunities for a
broader range of activities.

Dear Diary,

Another school day - I like school SO much!

Meilin + I fed the birds before school started at 8 o'clock.

Remember the story I wrote yesterday? I read it out to the class. Everybody liked it, 'specially Miss Siti.

During recess, I saw some friends from Pr. 5 and we played catching. Then one of the Pr. 6 girls read a story to us. Recess is more fun than last year when I was in Pr. 3 + had only 20 mins for recess.

My class collected some pond water today. We put a drop on a piece of glass (Miss Lee says it is a "slide") and looked at it under a microscope. Wow! There were so many stranger wriggly things! Imagine what a stomach ache I will have if I swallow some pond water!

In the after-school care group, Mrs Soh explained how to do two Maths sums I got for homework. She is patient. I also had an Art and craft lesson. Miss Lily is teaching us cross-stitch.

There is SO much to do in school, I feel sad when Papa comes to fetch me home.

Holidays begin tomorrow. I never have much to write then.

Goodnight!

Devi

"Neighbours In Close Encounter": this peer tutoring scheme at Bedok South Secondary is a good example of the strong helping the weak.

Smaller Class Size. We will also reduce class size. This will allow for a wider range of peer group activities and closer interaction. Teachers will be able to give more individual attention and pace the lessons to their pupils' needs.

Better Means and Ways for All. We will promote better methods of teaching and more interaction between teacher and pupil and also among pupils. We will provide richer curricula and more interesting and motivating learning materials, often using information technology. Schools will bring a multi-media approach to teaching and will develop efficient teaching tools.

Help for Some. Certain groups of pupils do less well than others. For those with learning difficulties, educational psychologists will work with schools in diagnosing and overcoming learning problems.

Community groups have stepped forward to give a helping hand. We applaud and support such efforts. For example, we are working together with Mendaki, in the Mendaki-MOE Committee, to set up programmes to

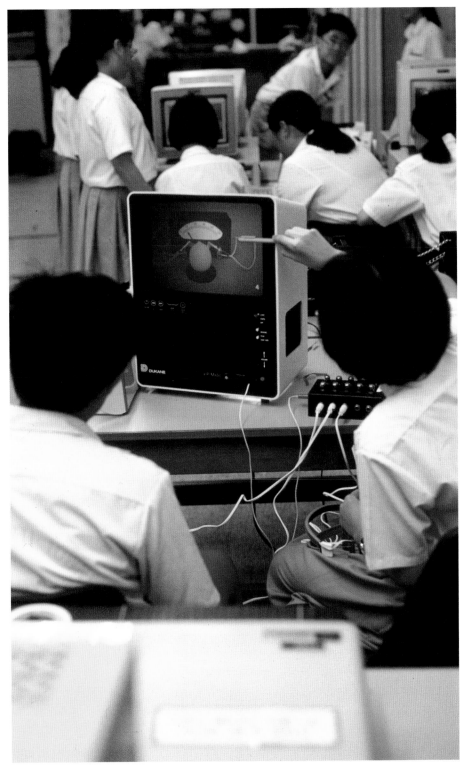

Technical equipment and computers are widely used in schools. In addition, Teleview gives students entrée to interactive programmes and illustrates well the principle of self-access learning.

There will be more choices for our children…and electives for those who have special talents.

Below: Secondary schools will introduce a pre-vocational course to prepare students for skills training.

help Malay children with their educational needs. Likewise, we will help other community groups, like the Singapore Indian Development Association (SINDA), which reach out to those who need help with their schoolwork.

For More Diversity. Some primary schools and more secondary schools will go independent. These will lead the way in educational improvements. They will provide for greater diversity and choice, and our education system will be the richer for it.

Developing Talents. There will be more choices to cater for the diversity of our children's talents. We will introduce a new course with a pre-vocational emphasis to prepare secondary students for skills training. This will direct their attention towards the technological challenges of industry. We will expand the Gifted Education Programme to allow more children who can benefit to participate. There will be electives for those who have special talents. These will include programmes in art, music, drama studies and foreign languages.

Students at sports and recreation: providing balance and developing camaraderie.

Overleaf: A Physical Education class at Tampines Junior College.

Maintaining Our Values. Our schools will not only push for higher levels of academic achievement. They will also keep alive our Asian values and traditions. Schools must, hand in glove with the home, produce morally upright, diligent and compassionate citizens. The teaching of civics and values will be improved and emphasized in the civics and moral education programme.

We need good, well-trained teachers. Here are some teachers discussing ideas and sharing their experiences with each other.

Below: Trainee teachers at work stations pick up computer skills.

Our Teachers

Our pupils spend at least 1,000 hours a year in constant contact with
teachers. Teachers play a fundamental role in society – shaping the thoughts
and moulding the character of future generations of Singaporeans. Hence,
teacher training is a serious undertaking which must be in step with
changing times.

Building a National Institute of Education. The new National Institute of
Education (NIE) will introduce a degree programme for primary school
teachers. It will offer better teacher training programmes. NIE will also
spearhead research in education.

Developing Teachers. Teacher centres will be set up to promote greater
professional awareness. In-service courses will be provided to upgrade the
skills of our teachers.

Our Tertiary Institutions

In the mid-1970s, about 9 per cent of a Primary One cohort went to
polytechnic or university. By the mid-1980s, this proportion had trebled to
27 per cent. This growing pool of graduates enabled Singapore to plug into
the high-tech industries and the information age.

   We will continue to meet the increasing demand for a higher-level,
multi-skilled workforce. In doing so, we will also satisfy growing aspirations
for tertiary education.

*Economic growth depends on
the quality of our technical
manpower. Polytechnics are
instrumental to the
development of industry.*

Polytechnics – Linking with Industries

In 1990, we established the third polytechnic, Temasek Polytechnic, to
complement existing programmes and broaden the range of options offered.
If demand increases further, more polytechnics will be built.

   The polytechnics' philosophy has been to maintain a close partnership
with industry. This has helped produce the skilled technicians and middle
management staff much sought after in the various economic sectors. As

Polytechnics focus not only on technical subjects but also on the aesthetics – graphic design and architectural drafting.

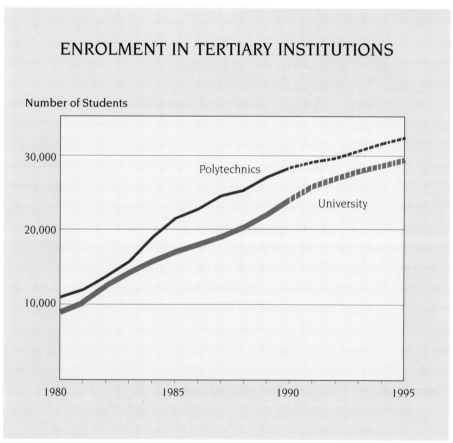

ENROLMENT IN TERTIARY INSTITUTIONS

Number of Students

the quality of technical education improves, the standing of our polytechnics will rise, and employers will give due recognition to their graduates.

University – Meeting Growing Needs

As school results improve from year to year, more young people will have the prerequisites to benefit from university education. We will create more university places to accommodate them in a greater range of disciplines.

By mid-1991, Singaporeans will have two full-fledged universities, competing and cooperating with one another. If the two universities grow too large, we will consider setting up a third university. This can either be another state-funded institution or a private university linked to a prestigious overseas institution.

Providing Opportunities. We will also consider the needs of those who could not obtain a university education in their earlier years. We will provide opportunities for these mature students for they deserve a second chance. Indeed, mature students can add depth to university life.

Broadening the Mind. Our universities will be in tune with the times, keeping an ear on what society expects of graduates and adapting their degree programmes. University lecturers will be cognizant with teaching methods. They will fulfil the university's mission to inspire and challenge the nation's finest minds.

Our tutors will develop not only the creative abilities of their students, but also the entrepreneurial spirit and the drive to broaden their minds and extend their vision. The universities will develop the potential of their outstanding undergraduates. They will offer double-discipline programmes to challenge and develop their multiple talents.

Forging Links. The universities will continue to seek out talented people in society – professionals, industrialists, administrators – who can share their experience with the students. This will form a bridge between the

"...the university's mission is to inspire and challenge the mind."

Final-year law students honing their persuasive skills in the moot court.

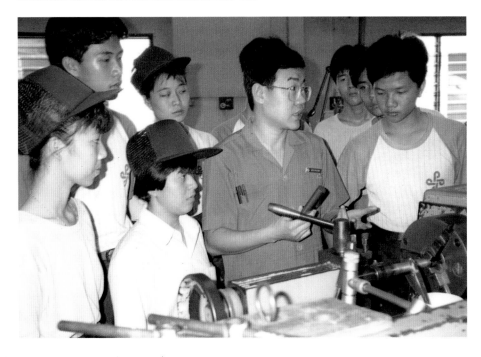

At post-secondary level, vocational institutes train skilled workers for our industries.

university and the workplace. University graduates must develop positive attitudes towards continued and further training. Just as skilled workers need new skills to cope with changing demands, graduates will need further training and education in new disciplines.

Skills Training

Work Ethics and Productivity. Our young people will eventually graduate and enter the workforce. It is crucial that they have good work ethics. The school, in tandem with the home, will instil and reinforce good personal habits which will lead to good work attitudes.

We will invest in vocational education. We will update and upgrade continually our vocational courses. Singapore's industrial future lies in the training and retraining of its workforce to meet changing demands.

Keeping in Step. Full-time, broad-based courses will continue to meet the demands of major industrial sectors. The Vocational and Industrial Training Board (VITB) will also work hand-in-hand with employers in its enhanced apprenticeship scheme, where trainees acquire practical skills at work and attend classes part-time.

"Singapore's industrial future lies in the training and retraining of its workforce to meet changing demands."

Continuing education for our workers: the NPB "Fast Forward" programme helps workers to keep upgrading their skills through self-access home-based learning.

Continuing Education – A Second Chance

Continuing education through part-time study or training will remain a feature of our education system. It will offer a chance for those who missed out in their earlier years. Apart from on-site courses, like those by the VITB institutes and the polytechnics, we will also experiment with programmes like Fast Forward, initiated by the National Productivity Board. These will be tailored for maximum flexibility, for well-motivated students to study at their own pace.

We will also use the media to offer a wide range of options for self-access learning. We will expand, especially, the role of Teleview to this area.

The universities will be part of the continuing education network and provide part-time undergraduate and postgraduate courses. We will explore the possibility of linking with established open university programmes, to provide opportunities for continuing learning at the degree level.

Special Education

We will continue to provide for children who have special needs. We will harness technological advances so that our disabled children may enjoy better educational facilities. Teachers in the special schools will be competently trained and backed up by specialist professional help.

Singapore must be a caring society. We will not exclude the disabled from the mainstream. Special schools will be located close to the normal schools to give disabled and normal children more opportunities to meet and play together. Parents of the disabled will be counselled in the education and training of their children. Employers too will be better informed of the capabilities of the disabled and be encouraged to give them fulfilling and appropriate employment.

Sharing Our Experiences

We must be conscious of the outside world, especially of our neighbours in ASEAN. We must get to know them, both as individuals as well as countries. We must build bridges between the peoples.

One way is to encourage some students from these countries to study in Singapore. They will form abiding friendships, and our students too will benefit from meeting foreign students with different backgrounds.

Edusave is an investment in our future.

We should therefore offer more places and scholarships to foreign students in our universities, polytechnics and schools. We will also explore the possibility of setting up a private regional school.

Edusave – Exercising Choice

Education is expensive. However, the long-term returns make the investment worthwhile. The government will raise its financial commitment to education from 4 per cent to 5 per cent of our GDP.

An Edusave account will be opened for every Singaporean schoolchild between the ages of 6 and 16. Into each account, we will contribute an annual sum. Parents too will be encouraged to contribute to their children's Edusave accounts. Throughout the period of their children's general

Extracurricular activities foster leadership, friendship and a sense of responsibility. They help to inculcate values in young people.

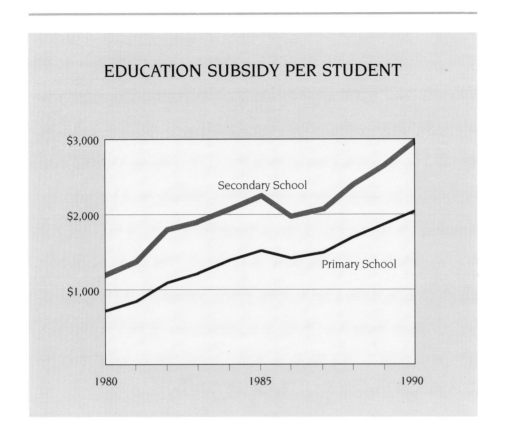

EDUCATION SUBSIDY PER STUDENT

education, parents can then use this account to pay school-related and school-supported course fees.

Thus, every school-going child between the ages of 6 and 16 will be given an additional educational subsidy to be utilized for enrichment, for remedial classes or to be saved for future education. Parents will make the choice.

Edusave is an investment in our children and in the future of Singapore.

Moving Towards Our Future

The future of a nation hinges on its vision. Our vision is to become a well-educated society.

We will take bold steps towards this vision. The broad-ranging plans cover pre-school to tertiary levels and continuing education. There will be opportunities for life-long learning so that Singaporeans can continue to develop. In this way, we will maximize the potential of each and every one, and thereby achieve excellence in education at every level and in every sphere.

"There will be opportunities for life-long learning so that Singaporeans can continue to develop...we will maximize the potential of each and every one..."

A *Second University*: NTU

July 1, 1991 will mark the beginning of a new chapter in university education. The Nanyang Technological Institute will become a full-fledged university in its own right, the Nanyang Technological University (NTU).

The Technology Arm. NTU will build on NTI's strengths. Its degree programmes in the Engineering disciplines, Accountancy and Business, and Applied Science will form the technology arm.

The Education Arm. The other arm will be the National Institute of Education. It will have degree programmes for teacher training and in the Humanities and Sciences.

Distinguishing Features. They will be industry-oriented. We will establish joint research and training centres. Industrial attachments will be an important feature.

There will be collaborative agreements with leading overseas institutions, similar to NTI's current links with the Mechanical Engineering Laboratory of Japan (MEL) and the MIT Sloan School of Business.

The Future. NTU is considering an American-British hybrid degree structure, which incorporates the American credit system but with a prescribed core curriculum. This will give more flexibility and greater choice. It will also explore the possibility of overseas student attachments to good American universities.

NTU may offer degree programmes in non-traditional areas like hotel administration and communications. It will collaborate with universities pre-eminent in these fields.

NTU will be a campus village for students, staff and the local community. As all students in the first and final years will stay on campus, enduring ties will be built for the future.

EDUCATION GOALS

- To maximize learning potential
- To develop thinking and creativity
- To nurture leadership qualities and good work ethics
- To cultivate civic and moral values

PRE-SCHOOL

- Expand preparatory year programme
- Support for pre-school education

SPECIAL EDUCATION

- Specialist teachers
- School Psychological Service
- Counselling parents

PRIMARY

- Single-Session/Day Schools
- Independent schools
- Educational psychologists
- Edusave
- School Psychological Service

THE TEACHING PROFESSION

- Elevate training programmes
- Upgrade in-service courses
- Spearhead research
- Teacher centres

SECONDARY

- Single-Session/Day Schools
- Pre-vocational courses
- Richer & more creative curriculum
- Edusave

SKILLS TRAINING

- Tailor programmes to meet the needs of industry
- Promote continuing education

TERTIARY

- Upgraded & expanded polytechnic diploma courses
- Promote inquiry & scholarship
- More flexibility and greater choice of programmes
- Third university

The Economy
Running The Next Lap

A ll our plans depend on strong economic growth. Over the past 25 years, Singapore has become a thriving modern economy, with the second highest standard of living in Asia. To reach the next milestone, Singaporeans will have to work hard, work smart, continuously hone our skills and simultaneously acquire new ones.

We should not allow the physical limits of our city-state and small population to constrain us. We cannot do everything, but we can be major players in a few key areas. By becoming a hub city, we can bring prosperity to the region and ourselves.

"All our plans depend on strong economic growth."

Winning the Team Relay

We compete in the race of nations, whether we like it or not. We have done quite well competing in the second league. The next step is to make it to the top league. Our competitors are already doing that. Unless we do the same, we shall be left behind.

"The next step is to make it to the top league."

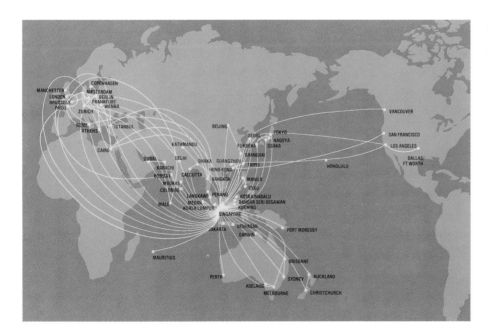

Singapore, a global hub.

SIMEX *is the first exchange in Asia to trade in financial futures.*

Opposite: The Port of Singapore, the largest single container terminal operator in the world, handles more than four million containers a year.

Our strategies for progress – free market principles, open competition, and rational economic policies – have served us well, and remain sound. For the next lap, we need in addition new strategies.

We must sustain and sharpen Singapore's competitive advantage. This advantage is not predestined. It is created, through imagination, dedication to excellence and teamwork.

Around the world, key economic activities are becoming concentrated in a few strategic nodes. In finance, the key centres are Zurich, London, New York, Tokyo, Hong Kong and Singapore. In shipping, Rotterdam serves Europe, Yokohama serves Japan, Hong Kong serves China, and Singapore serves a region stretching from India to Taiwan, and beyond. The same is happening in air transport, telecommunications, information technology, and even industries like chemicals and petrochemicals.

Each strategic centre attracts business from an extended hinterland, and prospers out of proportion to the size of the local economy. Each is a hub, servicing the region and linking it to the world. Each builds up its position by investing in its people, planning far ahead, organizing itself as a world-class team, and staying ahead of the pack.

"This [competitive] advantage is not predestined. It is created, through imagination, dedication to excellence, and teamwork."

Singapore has always been an entrepot, but a hub city is much more than an entrepot. A hub must offer first-class products and services. The infrastructure must rank with the best in the world. The quality of service must be acknowledged even by competitors. "Singapore" must become a synonym for quality, reliability and excellence. We will become a business hub of the Asia Pacific.

How Do We Get There?

Our People. We will invest heavily in our people, to enable them to move up to higher value added and hence better paid jobs. The key is higher productivity. Labour productivity must improve by at least 3 to 4 per cent per year for the next decade. We have moved from labour-intensive industries to skill- and knowledge-intensive industries and services. In the next lap, skills and knowledge will become even more crucial in determining winners and losers. We need to work smarter, be better organized and discover new work methods. We can achieve this through innovation, technology and teamwork.

Our workers have been consistently rated as Number One over the past

Information Technology (IT) in our offices improves productivity and business performance.

decade by BERI, the Business Environment Risk Information service. We rate high on productivity and industrial relations, but lower on technical skills. The World Competitiveness Report rates our workforce high on motivation, education and vocational training, but lower on the quality of skilled labour.

The younger workers have benefited from the new education system introduced in 1978. But 600,000 older workers have no secondary education. Three hundred and thirty thousand did not complete primary school. We will provide the means for them to upgrade their education and technical skills too, so that we can catch up with the developed countries. So far, 150,000 of them have attended BEST. Thirty thousand have enrolled for WISE. The government will work with the NTUC to enable more workers to attend the BEST, WISE and Fast Forward programmes.

Even skilled workers need post-employment training and on-the-job upgrading, to update what they have learnt in school. The Skills Development Fund will help companies increase their investment in training from the present 1.5 per cent of payroll to the 4 per cent which developed countries spend.

NTUC *and the Trade Unions.* We have enjoyed excellent labour management relations. Tripartite cooperation among the unions, employers and government has brought enduring industrial peace and contributed significantly to investor confidence. The trade unions, employers and bodies like the National Wages Council and the National Productivity Council must continue to foster better labour management relations.

The NTUC and its affiliated trade unions have played a pivotal role in our economic development. They have taken the lead to encourage workers to upgrade their skills and productivity. Their responsible and constructive attitude has set the tone for harmonious industrial relations in all sectors of the economy. This has enabled us to focus our energies on increasing the size of the economic pie, instead of dissipating them on fruitless disputes. Since independence, average pay has gone up eightfold.

Strong unions are important to Singapore. Not only must workers receive fair wages matching their productivity and output, they must also share in the success which they have helped to create. The government will ensure that the NTUC receives a fair share of resources and talent. It will set aside land for recreational facilities for union members, like the Pasir Ris Resort and the Orchid Country Club. It will support the Institute of Labour Studies, which will upgrade the leadership and management skills of unionists and workers.

"The NTUC and its affiliated trade unions have played a pivotal role in our economic development."

Developing our Infrastructure. Our airport, seaport, industrial parks, tele-communications network, and financial and convention facilities are the result of long-range vision and planning. Changi Airport is a good example.

Changi – Where the World Meets

From Paya Lebar to Changi Airtropolis. The Changi Airtropolis story is one example of how long-term planning can build up and sharpen a competitive advantage.

Paya Lebar Airport was still serving us well in the 1970s. But air traffic was growing steadily, and forecasts showed that it would eventually become too heavy for Paya Lebar to handle.

The government decided to build a new airport at Changi. It decided to write off not only the existing infrastructure at Paya Lebar, but another $700 million which would have to be spent expanding Paya Lebar pending the completion of Changi.

Six hundred and seventy hectares of land were reclaimed off Changi, creating enough space for three airport terminals and two runways. In 1981 Changi Airport opened with one runway. A second runway began operating in 1984. Terminal Two opened in 1990.

From the Best Airport to a Global Focal Point. The commitment, teamwork and professionalism of the airport team – the air traffic controllers, the counter staff, the baggage handlers, the immigration, customs and security officers – made Changi a success. Within seven years, Changi was voted the best airport in the world.

Changi has become one of the busiest airports in the region. Air traffic has doubled in 10 years. Fifty-four international airlines fly to Singapore. We are linked by more than 1,950 weekly flights directly to 109 cities.

Traffic should double again in the next 10 years. CAAS is already planning for Terminal Three. It is reclaiming yet more land off Changi, to cater for Terminal Four and a third runway. By the year 2000, Changi should be an aviation superhub – helping to make Singapore the meeting place of the world.

Changi Airport has been rated the world's best airport for the third consecutive year. The opening of Terminal 2 (opposite and preceding pages) is one more step towards improving our infrastructure and services.

The new Brani Terminal is the next step in making Singapore a premier maritime centre.

Below: The Cruise Centre will make Singapore the cruise gateway of the Asia Pacific.

We need to upgrade and automate our port operations to stay the busiest container port in the world. PSA needs to plan ahead 30, 40 years, to attract and handle 10 times the business it does today. This means a new port, either at Pasir Panjang or Tuas, or possibly on reclaimed land in the Southern Islands.

Many international traders use Singapore as a trading, financing, servicing and logistics hub. Billions of dollars of business is done through Singapore, often without the goods coming anywhere near us. As regional economies liberalize and new markets emerge, this trade will expand further.

Our telecommunications network offers IDD connections around the world at very low rates. The ISDN service transmits voice, data and images to several major countries. This international traffic will more than double by the year 2000. Telecoms will install high-capacity optic fibres, satellite links, submarine cables and new telephone switches to open up new avenues in broadcasting and communications. One day, we may even operate our own communications satellite.

Information is the lifeblood of the economy. Extensive use of

Integrated Services Digital Network (ISDN), allows for voice, data and video communications all on one line.

Below: The computer peripherals industry supplies both global and regional customers.

information technology will create smart physical infrastructure, from ports to roads to buildings. Tradenet handles trade documents quickly and cheaply. Globalink will provide on-line global trade information. Lawnet will provide on-line legal databases. Portnet will speed up port documentation, communications and operations. Teleview will bring information technology into the home. Such projects will transform Singapore into an "intelligent" island where diverse transactions can be effected instantaneously and efficiently.

We are already a regional data processing centre for MNCs. By improving the service infrastructure, Singapore will become a Total Business Centre, attracting MNCs, international investors, traders and talent.

Technology and Innovation. Some of our industries are major players in world markets, for example computer peripherals, petroleum refining, shipbuilding and repair, and oil rig construction. We are the largest producer of small format Winchester disk drives and tape drives, refrigerator compressors and some proprietary pharmaceuticals. MNCs have brought in state-of-the-art technologies – including wafer fabrication, product development

"Some of our industries are major players in world markets."

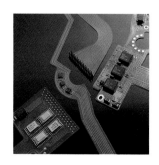

Singapore is the third largest oil refining centre in the world.

and design, computer integrated manufacturing systems and surface mount process technology.

For the next phase, we will have to be more focused in what we do. This means specializing and becoming leaders in specific niches, and doing more research and development. The National Science and Technology Board will promote R&D. In the Institute of Molecular and Cell Biology, 150 PhDs do basic research. The Institute of Systems Science and the Information Technology Institute conduct research in artificial intelligence and specialized computer software. We will be adding two more Institutes – for Microelectronics and for Manufacturing Technology.

We will foster the development of creative services. Nanyang Technological University will have an Institute of Technology and Design. An Academy for Creativity Training will be set up, comprising institutes for Communicative Arts, Designing Arts, Fine Arts and Performing Arts, plus a Creativity Development Centre.

Singapore has carved a niche for itself in orchids.

Below: The Institute of Molecular and Cell Biology.

Fashion design – a creative service.

Below right: Video production. Filmline Productions offers the only component video facility in Asia outside Japan.

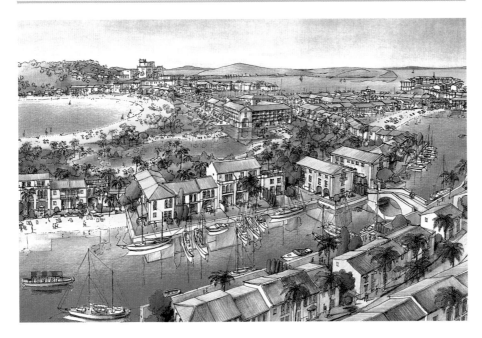

A *Quality Environment*. Economic and technological facilities are not enough. Talent is highly mobile. Our living and working environment must attract local and foreign talent to stay here. Sentosa and the Southern Islands will become world-class resorts for both Singaporeans and tourists. Science habitats, which combine quality living with research, design and other creative employment opportunities, will be set up. Community country clubs and the SAFRA clubs will be upgraded to meet higher aspirations.

"Our living and working environment must attract local and foreign talent to stay..."

Growth Triangle. The Growth Triangle links Singapore, Malaysia and Indonesia in a strategic partnership, sharing resources and capabilities. The arrangement helps all partners to grow faster together by combining what each has to offer – Indonesian factories with Singapore ports, Malaysian resorts with tourists from Singapore. The larger geographical area will offer investors a broader base for their operations, supporting their whole range of activities. For example, Sumitomo Electric is expanding its wire harness manufacturing operations in Batam and Johor, while maintaining technical support facilities in Singapore. Other companies like Smith Corona, Philips and Western Digital are also establishing integrated operations in the Growth Triangle.

"The Growth Triangle...helps all partners to grow faster together by combining what each has to offer..."

The first phase of the Batam Industrial Park is already full. Batam is developing an improved port, executive housing, and recreational facilities.

Bintan, with 18 kilometres of pristine beaches, is more suited to tourism, light industries and the development of water resources. A master plan for Bintan is ready. Land has been set aside for light industries. A 10,000-hectare joint tourism project is being developed on the northern coast.

Johor's infrastructure is more advanced. Many companies already have joint operations in Johor and Singapore. The Growth Triangle will improve further bilateral cooperation between Singapore and Johor.

International Linkages. We cannot do well by relying only on our own resources. Networking with other countries will generate mutual benefits and greater prosperity for all. Singapore companies must increasingly venture overseas and form international linkages. SIA has teamed up with Delta and Swissair to create a global aviation network. EDB's International Direct Investment programme helps local companies to invest overseas, spread their wings, and overcome the limitations of a small domestic market. SPH, F&N, Wearnes, Wah Chang, Yeo Hiap Seng, Keppel, Sembawang, Singapore Technologies Group, NatSteel and Singapore Telecoms International have done so. More should follow.

"Singapore
companies
must increasingly
venture overseas
and form
international
linkages."

Wearnes – Spreading Our Wings Abroad

- From a minor car dealer to a multifaceted global corporation
- From assembly of electronic components to R&D of integrated products
- From Singapore to the United States, United Kingdom, Norway, China, Japan...
- With sales from $74 million in 1983 to $900 million in 1990
- With 26 subsidiaries in 11 countries around the globe

Wearnes – a name linked to car distribution in the early 1980s. Within six years, a name in the Wall Street Journal 1989 Centennial Edition List of 66 global companies profiled as "A Selected Few Poised to Lead Business into the 1990s".

Faced with a limited domestic car market and spurred on by the government, Wearnes in 1984 sought global niches in information technology (both hardware and software), agrotechnology, biotechnology, specialized engineering, leisure and venture fund management. One of its acquisitions was Advanced Logic Research Inc, a leading company in the design and production of IBM compatible PCs.

"Whatever the strategy...we must remain flexible, adapt with the times, and be prepared to encounter surprises and seize opportunities by working together. This is the way to stay ahead in the next lap."

The Top League

We must not forget the fundamentals: a stable government, an honest and competent administration, national security, a system that is based on merit and rewards hard work and enterprise, and a commitment to excellence. Within this basic framework, the private sector can create wealth, and workers can benefit from growth. These strategies will prepare us for the top league.

No race turns out exactly as expected. Whatever the strategy, there will be unexpected problems, possibly upsets. We must remain flexible, adapt with the times, and be prepared to encounter surprises and seize opportunities by working together. This is the way to stay ahead in the next lap.

Singapore 2000 – Global Technopolis gave the Singapore public and business clients a glimpse of the future.

Singapore Our Home

An HDB *block and the children's park in* Pasir Ris *(opposite and above).*

The face of Singapore has changed dramatically over the past 25 years. Elegant glass-and-steel skyscrapers have taken the place of city slums. Highrise satellite towns have replaced fishing and farming villages. New parks, town gardens and modern amenities, including an efficient infrastructure and a comprehensive transportation network, have been put in place to serve an expanding economy.

Singapore's physical development will continue to be guided by the needs of a growing economy. But it will also be shaped by the changing aspirations and expectations of an increasingly affluent society. With these in mind, the Urban Redevelopment Authority (URA) has mapped out the Singapore Concept Plan (overleaf) to develop Singapore into a tropical city of excellence. We can look forward to a gracious living and working environment, comfortably accommodating a population of up to 4 million.

Singapore will be a modern city with world-class infrastructure and facilities, as well as a tropical island of fun and leisure. It will be a city that offers diversity and choice, a city with a rich variety of environments, a city of character and grace.

"[Singapore]...a city that offers diversity and choice, a city with a rich variety of environments."

Small can be Beautiful

Land is a precious resource. We must make the best use of it. If we reclaim land on the mainland and offshore islands to the limit, we can increase Singapore's land area by 15 per cent, equivalent to 12 Ang Mo Kio new towns plus 13 Botanic Gardens.

Our planning strategy is to carefully craft a rich and varied urban environment out of the land we have. Singapore will be a city with a world competitive infrastructure for commerce and industry. Singaporeans can expect quality housing, higher standards of health care, better educational facilities and a wider scope for sporting, recreational and cultural pursuits.

SINGAPORE CONCEPT PLAN

LEGEND

HIGH DENSITY HOUSING

LOW/MEDIUM DENSITY HOUSING

COMMERCIAL

INDUSTRY

BUSINESS PARK

OPEN SPACE/RECREATION

INFRASTRUCTURE

INSTITUTION

SPECIAL USE

LIVE FIRING AREA

CENTRAL AREA

MRT

LRT

N

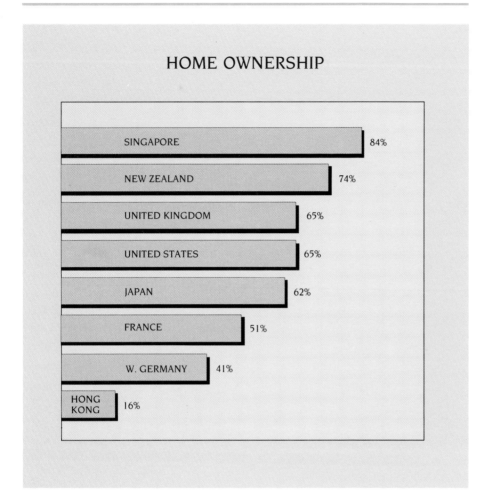

HOME OWNERSHIP

Country	Percentage
SINGAPORE	84%
NEW ZEALAND	74%
UNITED KINGDOM	65%
UNITED STATES	65%
JAPAN	62%
FRANCE	51%
W. GERMANY	41%
HONG KONG	16%

Opposite: Kampong Bugis, at the confluence of the Rochor and Kallang rivers, will be transformed into a pleasant living environment.

The People's City

With increasing affluence, the expectations of Singaporeans are rising. Already, 84 per cent of our people own the homes they live in compared to about 50 to 60 per cent in many developed countries. As the population increases, we will continue to encourage home ownership and improve the living environment. This we can do comfortably even with a population of 4 million.

Quality Homes. A wider choice of housing will be made available and new housing forms will be encouraged. More medium and low density housing, ranging from flats and condominiums to townhouses and landed properties, will be built. Some of these will be on prime locations such as along waterfronts.

"…we will continue to encourage home ownership and improve the living environment."

Simpang, a low-rise, waterfront town, will be built at the mouth of Sungei Seletar. It will have a rustic design reminiscent of the old kampong.

Simpang, at the mouth of Sungei Seletar, will be one such development. In the Development Guide Plan under preparation, Simpang will have a waterfront town centre, a bird sanctuary, marine recreational facilities, and beaches.

Buran Darat will be a smaller scale low density waterfront housing area, connected to both the recreation island of Sentosa and the mainland by the new Sentosa causeway. This project will be implemented in the next 5 to 10 years.

Sites next to parks and recreational areas will be set aside for housing. More housing will also be introduced within and near the central business district, for example, on prime sites at Kampong Bugis and Tanjong Rhu, and to capitalize on the views of Kallang Basin, Marina Bay, Rochor River and Geylang River.

Quality housing will be developed near academic and research institutions, high-technology industries and within business parks. These "science habitats", to be implemented by the end of the decade, will foster interaction among scientists, business people and the community at large.

The Upgrading Programme. Older HDB estates are not left out of this master plan to create a more pleasant and gracious living environment. A multi-billion dollar Upgrading Programme will improve the environs of these estates, and turn entire precincts into fine housing estates comparable to private developments. Common areas within each block will be made more attractive. Multi-storey garages will replace surface carparks, thus releasing open spaces for landscaping, playgrounds and other facilities. Residents can live, socialize and enjoy themselves in a much improved environment without having to move out of a familiar neighbourhood.

"The Upgrading Programme will turn entire precincts into fine housing estates comparable to private developments."

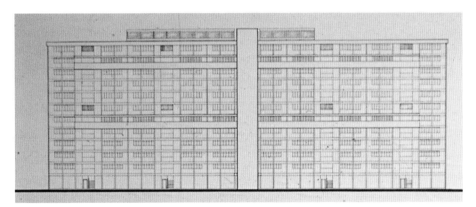

BEFORE

Upgrading the facade of an HDB block: before and after.

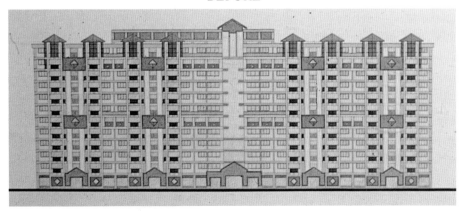

AFTER

A *quiet evening at home*. Although there will be more households, the standard of housing will continue to rise with bigger living space all round.

Higher Standards. In spite of the expected doubling of the number of households, the standard of future housing will be higher than that of today. Singaporeans now enjoy an average of 20 square metres of floor space per person. This is equivalent to a family of four living in a 3-room flat. Living area will be increased to about 35 square metres per person. A family of four can expect to live in a 4-room flat or better.

Business City

We can become a world centre for trade, finance, aviation and maritime services, information, business and manufacturing. To achieve this, we must be international in outlook. Our infrastructure must be as good as, if not better than, other major cities. Our city will keep pace with technological developments.

"Our infrastructure must be as good as, if not better than, other major cities."

A New Hub. A new city hub, aesthetically designed, will be developed to cater to expanding business in the city. This new centre, an extension of the present downtown district, wraps around the scenic Marina Bay, and

The new city hub which wraps around the scenic Marina Bay is an extension of today's downtown district. Taking full advantage of the waterfront setting, it will have, apart from office blocks, residential, shopping and recreational facilities.

will be landscaped to take full advantage of the waterfront setting. Apart from office blocks, there will be residential, shopping, recreational and other facilities to bring activity and life both day and night. We will see the first buildings completed in the new downtown by the year 2000.

Regional Centres. We will establish regional centres for commercial activities that do not need to be downtown. Each regional centre will be configured to provide a balance between jobs and homes, to reduce travelling time to and from work and ease congestion within the central business district. Three regional centres – Jurong East, Tampines and Woodlands – will be created over the next 10 years.

Business Parks. Existing industrial estates will be refurbished and updated. At the same time, new business parks will be developed to meet the needs of newer generations of information-based and high-technology industries. In these parks, workplaces and businesses will mesh with residential and recreational facilities.

The International Merchandise Mart, a wholesale marketing centre. It will be part of the regional business centre in Jurong East, which will house activities not requiring a downtown location.

Below left and bottom: The Singapore Science Park, our first R&D park, and the interior of the Compaq factory. They are precursors of future business parks.

Benjamin Sheares Bridge, the viaduct that spans the Kallang and Singapore rivers and connects the East Coast to the West Coast. More overpasses, underpasses and road tunnels will be built.

Overleaf: An MRT train passing through Yishun. The MRT system will be extended significantly.

Business parks will be developed on particular themes. By the year 2000, we will have an R&D business park in the Ayer Rajah/Rochester Park area next to the tertiary institutions, an aviation business park near Seletar Airbase, and a medical business park near the Singapore General Hospital.

Easy Transit

Providing easy transit is a challenge to major cities everywhere. Singapore has been able to contain the problem of city jams. We will continue to do so, while at the same time making commuting more comfortable and convenient.

Traffic. The present network of expressways and roads will be upgraded and expanded. More overpasses, underpasses and road tunnels will be built to ensure smooth traffic flow. Electronic road pricing and computerized traffic control systems will enable more Singaporeans to use the roads.

"Providing easy transit is a challenge to major cities everywhere. Singapore has been able to contain the problem of city jams."

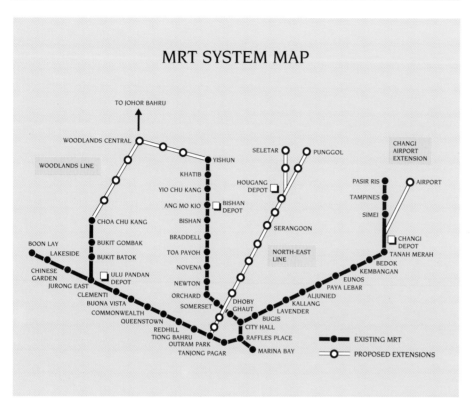

MRT SYSTEM MAP

TO JOHOR BAHRU

WOODLANDS CENTRAL

WOODLANDS LINE

SELETAR · PUNGGOL

CHANGI AIRPORT EXTENSION

YISHUN

KHATIB

YIO CHU KANG

ANG MO KIO

HOUGANG DEPOT

BISHAN DEPOT

PASIR RIS

TAMPINES

SIMEI

AIRPORT

CHOA CHU KANG

BISHAN

BRADDELL

SERANGOON

CHANGI DEPOT

TANAH MERAH

BOON LAY

LAKESIDE

BUKIT GOMBAK

BUKIT BATOK

TOA PAYOH

NOVENA

NORTH-EAST LINE

BEDOK

KEMBANGAN

EUNOS

PAYA LEBAR

CHINESE GARDEN

ULU PANDAN DEPOT

JURONG EAST

CLEMENTI

NEWTON

ORCHARD

ALJUNIED

BUONA VISTA

COMMONWEALTH

QUEENSTOWN

REDHILL

TIONG BAHRU

OUTRAM PARK

TANJONG PAGAR

SOMERSET

DHOBY GHAUT

KALLANG

LAVENDER

BUGIS

CITY HALL

RAFFLES PLACE

MARINA BAY

●━● EXISTING MRT

○━○ PROPOSED EXTENSIONS

Public Transport. Not every Singaporean can own a car, although many will. We will therefore develop alternative modes of public transport. Commuting will be made more comfortable. The MRT system will be extended to provide accessible, fast and comfortable public transport to more Singaporeans. Within five years, the MRT will be extended to Woodlands. In the longer term, possibly to Hougang and Punggol. The MRT system will be supplemented by light rail lines where feasible. More airconditioned buses will be added. The bus and MRT will be integrated to provide more convenient services. In time, the MRT may even take us to Johor Bahru.

Walkways and Malls. A good system of walkways and pedestrian malls is being developed in the city centre to encourage Singaporeans to walk rather than drive short distances. These pedestrian walkways will be well shaded with trees and plants, or even covered, to make them more comfortable to use in our hot and humid climate.

The tree-shaded pedestrian walkway at Handy Road near Cathay cinema. More such walkways and malls will be developed in the city centre to encourage Singaporeans to walk short distances rather than drive.

Environment City

We will aim for high standards of environmental quality and public health. Clean, healthy and aesthetic conditions everywhere will be the norm expected by every Singaporean. We will continue to upgrade standards of environmental management and instil in Singaporeans a national commitment to protect and preserve the local and global environment.

A City of Culture and Grace

We will be a city of culture and grace, where, after the day's work is done, we can look forward to a variety of cultural, recreational and sporting activities.

Green lungs in the city provide breathing space in between the urban concrete.

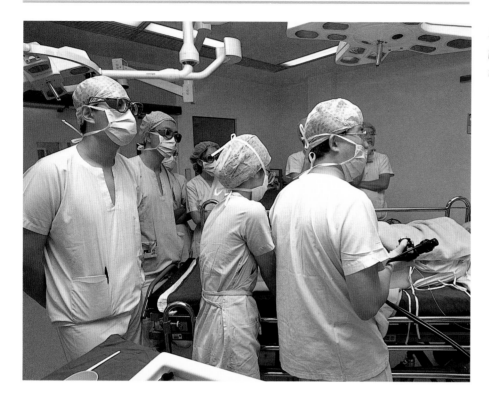

Medical and health care facilities will be redeveloped to meet changing needs.

Social Care. Existing medical and health care facilities will be redeveloped to meet changing needs. New facilities such as polyclinics and community hospitals will be built in new residential areas. A high standard of health care will be affordable and available to all.

Schools, where we nurture our young, will be better planned and have better facilities. We want to provide our young with the best possible learning environment.

Sports and the Outdoors. We will continue to encourage sports as a life-long pursuit and foster in our young a love for the outdoors. To keep themselves fit and robust, Singaporeans will have easy access to swimming pools, tennis courts, squash courts, golf courses, jogging tracks, sports stadiums and other sporting facilities. Being an island with easy access to the coast, we will further develop our seafront for water sports. There will be more beaches and marinas. The Southern Islands will be developed into recreational resorts offering waterfront chalets, resort hotels and marine recreational facilities in natural and idyllic settings for local and overseas visitors.

Shall we picnic at the beach
or go riding in the park?

Overleaf: For nature
lovers, wooded areas, bird
sanctuaries and mangrove
swamps.

The Darul Aman Mosque in Eunos. Land will be set aside for places of worship in new residential areas.

Kampong Glam with its majestic Sultan Mosque and rich cultural heritage will be conserved.

Below: The century-old late Victorian-style Singapore Cricket Club is a perfect foil to the skyscrapers behind it.

Even as our population is growing, we will put aside more open spaces and green areas. Parks with different themes and open spaces, scattered throughout the island, will be connected by a network of continuous green trails for jogging, cycling and other forms of recreation. This network, linking the parks to coastal areas, will make the whole of Singapore a "playground". Relatively unspoilt offshore islands, such as Pulau Ubin, will be kept for adventure parks, rock climbing and other rugged activities.

We will conserve some of our natural environment for nature lovers and to help us appreciate our rich and diverse surroundings. Wooded areas, bird sanctuaries and mangrove swamps will provide a welcome change to the urban environment.

Cultural Pursuits. With growing affluence and maturity come greater yearnings for the finer things in life. We will widen the scope for cultural pursuits by developing arts centres and libraries. A Singapore Arts Centre will be built at Marina Centre within the next decade. It will become the focal point for cultural activities in Singapore. We will become a hub for world-class cultural and artistic performances drawing both talent and audiences from the whole region, just as New York and London draw talent and audiences from the world.

Some buildings of historical and architectural merit will be conserved and put to good use as art galleries and museums. A large part of the Civic District will be designated as a museum precinct to accommodate a new museum complex and other cultural facilities. Projects in the Civic District and along the Singapore River will also be completed this decade.

A City For All Seasons

Singapore will be a city of diversity and richness in which intensive urbanization is balanced with the natural environment. Green spaces, hills, the sea, beaches and rivers will be carefully woven into the urban fabric. Scenic coastal roads will link with the main transportation network. There will be broad tree-lined boulevards leading into the city centre.

New complexes will provide modern services to support the economy. But we will also conserve and preserve old buildings that add to the character of our city and give us a sense of place and history. These old buildings, together with new monuments, pocket parks and wide boulevards, will contrast with ultra-modern skyscrapers to make our city visually exciting.

Singapore our home will be a city that is pleasant to live and work in, a city which has something to offer everyone, whether resident or sojourner.

"Singapore...will be a city that is pleasant to live and work in, a city which has something to offer everyone, whether resident or sojourner."

Arts and Sports
The Other Dimension

Ang Peng Siong, one of
the fastest swimmers in
Southeast Asia.

Singaporeans now aspire to the finer things in life – to the arts, culture and sports. At the same time, there is a call to preserve and explore our rich multicultural heritage.

The high level of attendance at both foreign and local performances during the 1990 Festival of Arts and at other cultural events, and the increasing popularity of sports like squash, tennis, swimming and windsurfing are signs of the desire for a more fulfilling life. This yearning has to be satisfied and it is in our national interest to do so.

Opposite: The Singapore
Dance Theatre gives a
modern interpretation to a
local dance.

Why Arts and Sports

The arts and sports appeal to our human spirit. Through the arts, we interpret life and explore our inner self. Through sports, we rejuvenate and renew ourselves, discover our limits and test the strength we can draw from our inner reserves. Together, they challenge us and imbue us with a zest for life. Indeed, it is through our myriad cultures, artistic expressions and sport pastimes that our people discover themselves, their history and their roots.

Arts and sports are vehicles, not only for the expression of the self, but also for communion with our fellow men. Our people are enriched and their sensibilities refined.

Hallmark of Great Cities. One hallmark of great cities is the abundance and quality of artistic, cultural and sport activities they support. We can provide the infrastructure; the life and vitality must come from our people.

For Singapore to grow into a hub for arts and sports, we must develop local talent and draw in regional and international talent. We will cultivate in our children an appreciation of the aesthetic and a love for sports. Singapore will be a good place to live in and people the world over will want to come, not only to visit, but also to work, invest and stay.

"We can provide
the infrastructure;
the life and vitality
must come from our
people."

The Singapore Arts Centre
will be built on the shores of
Marina Bay.

Below: Art at the
community level – HDB
void deck mural.

Realizing our Vision for the Arts

Our Asian Heritage. Our Asian arts make us unique and we must continue
to promote them in the face of more modern and western influences. We
need our cultural moorings, a perspective on our past. Singaporeans will
have opportunities to cultivate expression in the Asian arts and to integrate
our past heritage with present influences.

Centres for the Arts. Our cultural facilities will be improved and increased so
that better quality performances and exhibitions can be staged with greater
frequency. At the hub will be the Singapore Arts Centre which will be built
before the end of this decade at Marina Centre. With its acoustically
designed auditoriums and other related arts facilities, the Singapore Arts
Centre will be the focal point of cultural life in Singapore.

To complement the Singapore Arts Centre, existing theatres like the
Kallang Theatre, Victoria Theatre and Victoria Concert Hall will continue
to be upgraded. Companies will also be encouraged to allocate space for
the performing arts when designing their new buildings. Thus performances
can be hosted in convention spaces and auditoriums.

Empress Place (left) where collections from all over the world are exhibited. Peranakan Place (below): a glimpse into the daily life of the Straits Chinese. House museums allow us to appreciate the lifestyle of our forefathers.

Art at the Community Level. We will restore various vacant buildings to be used by cultural groups as rehearsal and working spaces, and incorporate them into conservation schemes. We will set up house museums in historical areas like Chinatown, Kampong Glam, Little India and by the Singapore River. Our heritage should blend with the present and remind us that arts and culture are the living expression of our nation.

Art will be brought to the community level. Works of art placed in public parks and buildings will not only create an aesthetic ambience but also instil a love of art in Singaporeans.

"Art will be brought to the community level."

The Museum Precinct. A Museum Precinct, around the foot of Fort Canning, will comprise a Fine Arts Gallery in the former St Joseph's Institution building, a Children's Museum in the former Tao Nan School building, a History of Singapore Museum in the present National Museum building, a Southeast Asian Ethnology and Natural History Museum and a People's Gallery.

The Fort Canning Museum Precinct will be the centre of the historical and cultural heritage of our nation. Our museums will be more than

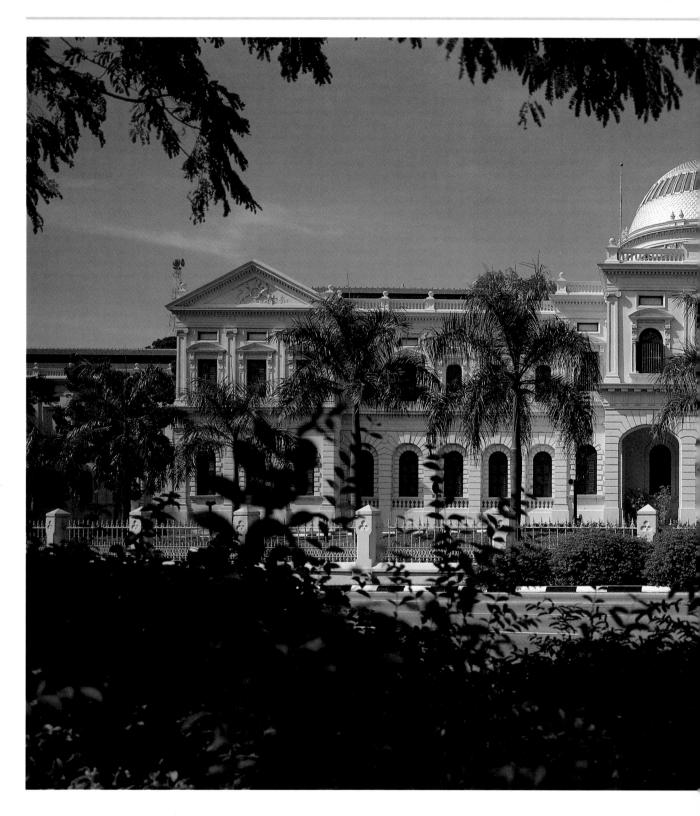

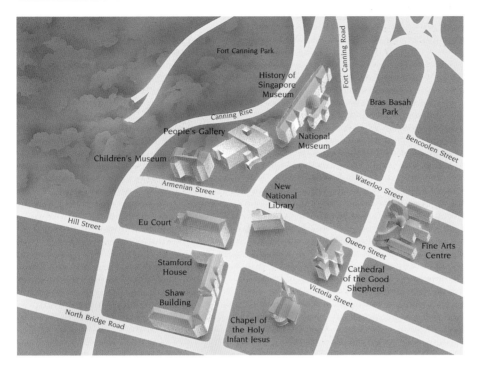

The Fort Canning Museum Precinct (left) will be the historical centre of Singapore with the National Museum (preceding pages) at its heart.

Below: More branches of the National Library will be built in the new towns.

repositories of cultural knowledge. They will mount programmes to promote greater understanding and appreciation of our culture and of the arts.

Nurturing the Reading Habit. Attention will also be given to the literary arts and to promoting the reading habit. Singaporeans will increasingly be better informed and well-read. We will read, not just because we must, but for self-fulfilment, to broaden our minds and deepen our sensitivities. By 1995, a modern and bigger National Library building will stand at the former site of Raffles Girls' School in Queen Street. It will incorporate the latest technology and facilities for modern and efficient library service. In addition, over the next five years, four new branch libraries will be constructed in Yishun, Tampines, Hougang and Woodlands.

Developing the Film Industry. Movies are an established art form. As our audiences become more selective, more multiplex cinemas will cater to their varied and discerning tastes. Our International Film Festival will become a major cultural event. It will include works of our film industry. The growth of this industry will create spin-offs in support areas. These will provide avenues for work and artistic expression for the more creative

"We will read…for self-fulfilment, to broaden our minds and deepen our sensitivities."

Going to the cinema: a favourite pastime of Singaporeans. The Picturehouse, the newest cinema in town, screens art films.

Author Philip Jeyaretnam

Photographer and Cultural Medallion winner Chua Soo Bin

Potter Iskandar Jalil,
Cultural Medallion winner,
at work.

Choreographer Goh Choo San

among us. Our censorship standards will also be updated, to give maximum freedom for artistic expression without offending decency and good taste.

The New Arts Council. The Singapore National Arts Council will be set up to oversee cultural activities and quicken their pulse and tempo. More resources will be mobilized to enliven the arts scene and make the arts more accessible to the community.

*We should build on our
Asian artistic heritage.
The confluence of various
artistic legacies makes
Singapore unique.*

Calligrapher Pan Shou

The Substation (left) experiments with the arts: where East meets West.

Below: Activities in schools and in artistic centres will develop skills in the arts and cultivate appreciation and participation.

Painter Thomas Yeo

Cyclist Kenneth Tan

Realizing our Vision for Sports

Sports for All. "Sports for All" will continue to be our national policy. Physical education programmes in schools will develop the physical abilities of our children and inculcate in them a love of sports. All Singaporeans will have more opportunities and facilities to take part in physical activity to keep them fit and robust.

More Opportunities. We will help to create and sustain the continued growth of sports. Both private and public sector employers and the mass media will be encouraged to support mass participation and excellence in sports.

In our schools, Physical Education (PE) and extracurricular activities (ECA) programmes have been revised to give greater emphasis to the

Acquiring healthy habits from young helps us to enjoy life to the full.

"All Singaporeans will have more opportunities and facilities to take part in physical activity to keep them fit and robust."

acquisition of sports skills and lifetime enjoyment of sports. We will promote especially sports which Singaporeans are likely to excel in, so that more can do well. Outstanding sportsmen and sportswomen will be given opportunities to realize their potential. The Singapore Armed Forces, too, will continue to support our national sport efforts.

Pursuing Adventure. To encourage the spirit of adventure, a new adventure centre, Outward Bound Singapore (OBS), will be completed on Pulau Ubin by end-1993. There, young Singaporeans can realize their physical and mental potential by overcoming unfamiliar obstacles and challenges and learn the importance of teamwork in the face of adversities.

Lee Wung Yew, Sportsman of the Year 1989

Sports in Singapore:
a mix of East and West.

Opposite: The Outward
Bound School – for a more
robust society.

Mass participation in the Singapore Marathon (left).

Below: Fresh air and exercise for healthy living.

Bowler Adelene Wee

Sports – A Way of Life. Singapore is well endowed with sports and recreational facilities. Soon, more will be available. Singaporeans will have even better access to swimming pools, stadiums with track and field facilities, badminton, squash and tennis courts. There will also be specialized facilities like artificial hockey pitches and Olympic gymnasiums.

Our aim is to promote a healthy lifestyle and to make sports a way of life for all Singaporeans.

Attaining the Other Dimension

Our vision is of a dynamic, culturally vibrant and physically robust society. We have a blueprint for developing Arts and Sports. We have the commitment and we will provide the investment. We can make this vision a reality.

"Our vision is of a dynamic, culturally vibrant and physically robust society."

Kite-flying, for some an art and for others recreation.

Many Helping Hands

M any helping hands is the Singapore Way of helping that small segment of our community who cannot keep pace with the rest of the population. They are found in every society, however affluent and progressive. Such families lag behind the rest of the population. They are in danger of becoming destitute, despite a comprehensive social security net in the form of the Central Provident Fund Scheme which provides protection in old age, major illness, incapacity and premature death of a breadwinner.

A *staff member of the Movement for the Intellectually Disabled attending to her charge.*

Opposite: Singaporeans contribute their bit to the Sharity Gift Box.

Who Are They?

They are low income families who have chronic physical, social, psychological or economic difficulties.

The Committee on Destitute Families Report (1989) classified them into two groups – the destitute families and the low income families vulnerable to destitution.

The destitute families number about 1,300 (or 0.3 per cent of total households). These families share the following characteristics:

- They have an income below subsistence level.
- The head of the household has dependent children and no means of support.
- The principal wage earner or family member is suffering from chronic disease, physical, intellectual or mental disability and faces hardship.
- They are elderly persons or couples above the age of 60 who have no relatives or means of support.

Those with very low incomes comprise some 22,000 families (or 3.5 per cent of total households). Equipped with little education and few skills, they are least able to adjust to rapid economic and technological changes. The death of a principal wage earner, a severe illness or personality disorder afflicting the head of household or other key family members, can spell destitution for the rest of the family.

"Many helping hands is the Singapore Way of helping those who cannot keep pace with the rest of the population."

Our Philosophy

Our Asian proverb, "It is better to teach them to fish than to give them fish", best illustrates our way of helping such families. This approach encourages the families to stand on their own feet and helps preserve their dignity and self-esteem.

We believe that children are our best hope for the future. We must give them every opportunity to succeed. We will pay particular attention to children from disadvantaged backgrounds and help them break out of the poverty trap. If they succeed, their parents succeed as well through them.

Thus, parents of disadvantaged children must help the government help their children. They must give their children all the care and attention

"It is better to teach them to fish than to give them fish..."

"This approach... helps preserve their dignity and self-esteem."

The Wishing Well, one of many 25th Anniversary Charity Fund activities.

A *nun from a Buddhist welfare organization provides a helping hand.*

Below: A *student receives a bursary award.*

"Investing in the education of children of low income families is the best way to help them break out of the poverty trap."

possible. If they keep their families small, they will have more resources to devote to each child.

We encourage many helping hands: from the government, corporate citizens, community organizations, religious groups, voluntary groups, concerned citizens and family members. All have a part to play and can do their bit to help the poor and disadvantaged. Together, we can grow as a compassionate and caring society.

Our Programmes

Helping the Children. We will emphasize helping the children of low income families. New generations of Singaporeans should not start life disadvantaged. Investing in the education of children of low income families is the best way to help them break out of the poverty trap. Various assistance schemes are already available to children in the schools and at constituency level, and more will be done to help them. The assistance given in the school ranges from bursaries and exemption from school, supplementary and examination fees to pocket allowances, and free textbooks, uniforms and milk.

Volunteers taking children on an outing.

Edusave. The Edusave scheme will provide additional help to children of lower income families to continue their education. Under this scheme, an annual grant will be given to every Singaporean schoolchild between the ages of 6 and 16. Parents will be able to use this government contribution to pay for their children's school-related course fees.

Edusave is our way of equalizing opportunities for each new generation.

Student Welfare Fund. We will help schools and their School Advisory or Management Committees to do more for socially disadvantaged children. A new scheme will give schools an initial grant to start a Student Welfare Fund. This is in addition to the Welfare Funds already set up by advisers of the Citizens' Consultative Committees in the constituencies to help needy children. We will match the funds raised by the school for the Student Welfare Fund dollar for dollar. Education loans and bursaries will also be more readily available.

Before and After School Care Services. For parents holding full-time jobs, BASC (Before and After School Care) programmes will help meet their child care needs. A network of BASC programmes is already being developed in centres run by voluntary welfare and community organizations and in some schools. When all primary schools go single-session, every school will be able to provide this service.

Children at a latch-key centre (above) and at a child care centre (left) while their parents work.

An employment scheme helps a youth find a job.

Opposite: Teenagers share their experiences during a group therapy session.

Counselling the Parents. Parent education programmes will be intensified to help parents help their children, particularly those in school. They are intended to help maintain stable family relationships and keep families intact.

Helping the Employable

Training and Job Placement. We will give priority to programmes which help the lower income families to acquire skills and hold down a job. We will organize a scheme to provide motivational attitude training to employable persons, apprentice them with companies with a view to job placement, and upgrade their skills to enable them to get better paid jobs.

All these programmes will be developed with the collective help of the government, statutory boards, companies and voluntary organizations. They will complement the existing counselling programmes, vocational training and job placement schemes of the government and voluntary workers' organizations.

Financial Assistance and Counselling

Rent and Utilities Assistance Scheme. Financial assistance is given only selectively. A new scheme to provide financial assistance to low income families who cannot pay their HDB rents and PUB bills was implemented in October 1990 through the Singapore Council of Social Service (SCSS) and its affiliates. An important component of this scheme is the counselling and assistance given to families to motivate them to pay their bills regularly on their own.

Family Service Centres. A network of Family Service Centres is being set up in the constituencies to provide advice and supportive help to families in need. They will also mount public education programmes on parenting and family life.

"We will give priority to programmes which help the lower income families to acquire skills and hold down a job."

Day care services help families take care of aged dependants.

Public Assistance Allowance. We will continue to make cash grants in the form of Public Assistance allowances to destitutes who have neither resources of their own nor friends or relatives who can help them.

Care and Shelter

Health Care. In Singapore, the poor will never be denied health care. Our restructured hospitals and polyclinics will continue to waive hospital fees and medical charges for the poor and indigent. Others can choose hospitalization wards according to their ability to pay. But they will enjoy equal standards of professional medical treatment, whatever their choice.

"The poor will never be denied health care."

MUIS volunteers help and comfort residents of the Woodlands Home for the Aged.

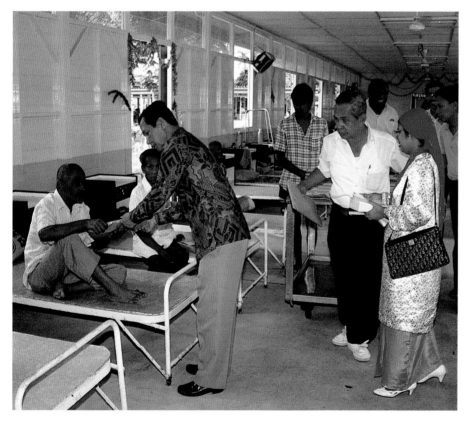

Young befriending the old.

Below: Senior citizens enjoying a game of gate-ball.

Child Care. Where families need to work, subsidized child care facilities are available. Parents who for one reason or another are unable to take charge of their children are also helped through a Fostering Scheme. Under this scheme, which covers both normal and disabled children, children are looked after by foster mothers in a normal home environment.

Community Care. No one in Singapore needs to beg. No one needs to live in the raw. We have homes which take care of the destitute, the aged poor, the severely disabled, children who are abused and children in need of care and protection.

Care for the Disabled. Special schools for disabled children will continue to get financial and professional support from the government. The Community Chest of Singapore, which also provides financial assistance, and the voluntary welfare organizations which run these schools will provide the other pairs of helping hands.

Learning to communicate on a Braille machine at the Singapore Association of the Visually Handicapped.

Left: Faster than jogging! Wheelchair athletes warm up.

Community Assistance

Spirit of Gotong Royong. We encourage the spirit of Gotong Royong, our local brand of community self-help. Already the community organizations have spearheaded a number of welfare programmes for the community and the needy. The bursary and welfare funds of the Citizens' Consultative Committees and other community organizations are examples. Residents' Committees also give help to families in their neighbourhoods in this same spirit of self-help.

The Citizens' Consultative Committees, Community Centre Management Committees, Residents' Committees and other community and civic organizations will widen their scope of voluntary service to meet the changing needs and aspirations of Singaporeans. More community and family clubs will be set up to foster a sense of belonging and community spirit, and reach out to all residents in the constituencies.

We all have a part
to play to help the
poor and disadvantaged.
Singaporeans must
help one another – the
Singapore Way.

Spirit of Voluntary Service. Some Singaporeans volunteer their time, money and ideas to help others in need. But the pool of volunteers is still small. Much more can and will be done to reach out to others who have the capacity to help.

Community Spirit. A good example of the many helping hands approach is the 25th Anniversary Charity Fund set up to commemorate Singapore's 25th Anniversary of Independence. The Fund is used for programmes and services to help low income families and others who require welfare assistance. Every segment of the population played its part and contributed to the Fund.

The Community Chest of Singapore and the National Kidney Foundation are other examples of the many helping hands approach in coming to the aid of the needy.

A Humane Society – The Singapore Way

Ultimately, we believe this is better than increasing taxes and leaving the government to be the sole provider for the welfare of the people. We believe in equalizing opportunities for each new generation. We believe in a compassionate society where Singaporeans look after each other. It is the Singapore Way.

The 25th Anniversary Charity Fund

The 25th Anniversary Charity Fund is a good example of the many helping hands approach to helping destitutes and low income families. A People's Fund raised by the people for the benefit of the people, it allowed for maximum involvement of all Singaporeans.

The Fund received overwhelming response from all sectors of the community. Donations ranged from a few cents to millions of dollars and far exceeded the target of $25 million. The Fund closed with $88 million which the government matched dollar for dollar.

Many innovative, creative and fun ways were used to raise funds. These included a musical wishing well and world record-breaking events such as the longest human centipede and largest bottlecap pyramid. On a cold wintry day in New Zealand, a wheelchair-bound Singaporean student raised over $200,000 in a 12-hour wheelathon. Grandparents and parents donated on behalf of their young children to set an example.

Heartrending examples included a father who pledged $50 in memory of his daughter who had recently died of liver failure. A 13-year-old schoolboy pledged $149.65 in memory of his uncle who passed away on the day he was born. A businessman pledged $50 for each day his baby, who had a hole in his heart, remained in the hospital.

The success of the Charity Fund exemplifies our compassion and care for the less fortunate.

The world's longest human centipede – an innovative way of raising funds.

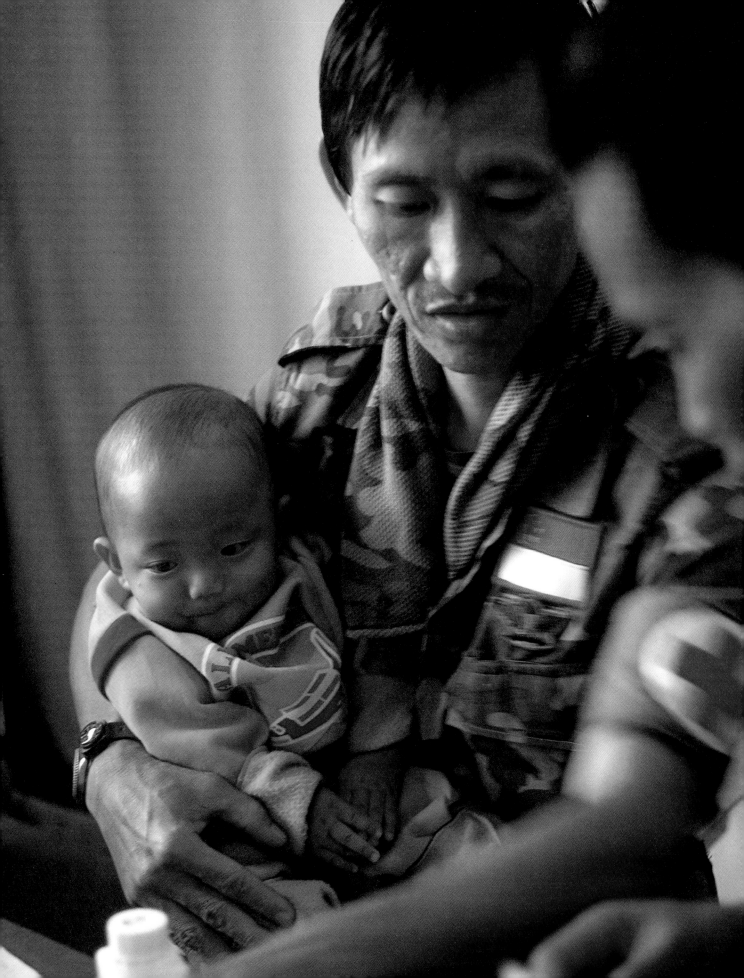

Singapore International

Singapore has always been plugged into the world. Our fortunes are inextricably linked by trade and commerce to the rest of Southeast Asia and to the international economy.

There is no other way we can grow and prosper. Technology has made this an interdependent world, a smaller world. Talent has become internationally mobile. This means new challenges and new opportunities.

More Singapore companies will be encouraged to spread their wings overseas. Growth triangles, involving the complementary use of resources across borders, will be encouraged. We want to be a business hub of the Asia Pacific and a hub for learning, the arts and culture.

As we become more international in outlook, we should at the same time remain Singaporean in heart and mind. We can learn from the experiences of other countries in fostering close ties between their compatriots abroad and the homeland. To help organize the Singaporeans who are overseas, we will establish the Singapore International Foundation.

Singapore International Foundation

The Singapore International Foundation will be a non-governmental organization. It will have an international advisory committee comprising friends of Singapore who are well respected both locally and abroad. Their wide-ranging expertise will guide the Foundation.

Forging International Links. The Foundation will be our vehicle to bring Singapore closer to Singaporeans overseas, ex-Singaporeans and friends of Singapore around the world. It will help nurture a Singaporean consciousness among overseas Singaporeans, mainly through overseas Singapore clubs.

Fostering International Goodwill. The Foundation will help promote international goodwill. One of its immediate tasks will be to publish a magazine for distribution overseas so that Singaporeans overseas and friends of Singapore can stay tuned. The Foundation will also organize a

Singapore's ambassador to the United Nations, Dr Chan Heng Chee, addressing the UN General Assembly.

Opposite: An SAF medical orderly, on Operation Lion Heart, attending to a baby in Baguio after the 1990 Philippines earthquake.

"The Singapore International Foundation will be our vehicle to bring Singapore closer to Singaporeans overseas…"

Lee Pan Hon, a violinist now living in England, returns occasionally to perform (left). Tang Da Wu, a performance artist who came home after many years overseas (below). W.C. Cheng, who returned from the United States, was the first private medical practitioner to develop an IVF (in vitro fertilization) programme (opposite, top).

"The Foundation will encourage foreign talent to work here...[and] support talented Singaporeans who want to perform or give exhibitions abroad."

corps of Singapore volunteers to work in developing countries. In a small way, we will make our contribution to the less fortunate in this world.

Gaining International Experience. The Foundation will encourage foreign talent to work here. It will identify Singaporeans who have distinguished themselves abroad. They will be invited home, to teach, to perform, to advise or, perhaps, to stay permanently.

The Foundation will help local institutions link up with their counterparts elsewhere. It will also support talented Singaporeans who want to perform or give exhibitions abroad.

Singaporeans Overseas

Singaporeans must look outwards and be prepared to live and work abroad. We must venture beyond our shores.

Working Abroad. Singaporeans working in other countries are not just exporting their services. They are ambassadors of Singapore. They can do much to promote goodwill and build up a positive image of Singapore internationally.

Already a small number of Singapore professionals and managers work overseas for multinational corporations and larger Singapore companies. To help Singapore companies expand overseas, Singaporeans will be encouraged to work abroad and to treat overseas postings as part of their personal and career development.

"Singaporeans must look outwards ...and be prepared to live and work abroad."

The Yeo Hiap Seng factory in Mauritius.

Education for Overseas Singaporeans. Singaporeans who work overseas often worry about their children's education. The Foundation will set up overseas Singapore schools and make other educational arrangements for them. This will make it easier for Singaporean children accompanying their parents overseas to fit into the Singapore education system when they return. The first overseas Singapore school will be set up in Hong Kong this year.

Links with Overseas Singaporeans. Since the 1970s, overseas Singaporeans have formed Singapore clubs in Hong Kong (1974), Los Angeles (1979) and San Francisco (1979). More recently, clubs were formed in London (1988), Sydney (1989), Vancouver (1989) and other cities. The Singapore International Foundation will work through these clubs to maintain ties with Singaporeans living abroad and with friends of Singapore. Through

Singaporean children at school in Hong Kong. A Singapore school in Hong Kong will soon be built for them.

Singapore's then ambassador to the UN, Professor Tommy Koh, chairing the UN Conference on the Law of the Sea (left), and participants of the Japan-ASEAN Regional Training Programme 90, on a field trip (below).

these ties, we hope overseas Singaporeans will retain their Singaporean identity and consciousness. They are a part of Singapore International.

An International City of Distinction

We are part of the global family of nations. As we become more developed, our responsibilities grow. We will play our part, however small, to make this a better world.

"We will play our part, however small, to make this a better world."

International Relations. Singapore will play its part to make this a safe, peaceful and prosperous world. Singapore will participate actively in international organizations like the United Nations, GATT, the Commonwealth, the Non-Aligned Movement and APEC.

This may include taking part in UN missions when called upon to do so. For example, we sent a police contingent to be part of the United Nations Transition Assistance Group (UNTAG) in Namibia in 1989. Or we may offer assistance in humanitarian and relief efforts.

Technical Assistance. Our policy of providing technical assistance to developing countries with which we have close bilateral relations will continue. Besides the existing ASEAN Technical Assistance Programme and the Colombo Plan, a programme will be developed with Japan to train

Members of Singapore's police contingent to the UN Transition Assistance Group in Namibia in 1989.

"...we aspire to be a society that is open and open-minded, thinking and acting as part of the world community of nations..."

technical personnel for third countries. If it proves successful, similar joint programmes will be initiated with other countries.

We will also offer technical assistance in areas where we have some comparative advantage. These include port management, communications, housing, urban redevelopment, health, education and the environment.

Going Further. We will think of new ways to make a contribution to the world and to the region in which we live. One way is to create additional places in our schools, polytechnics and universities for foreign students. Singapore has always been an education centre and an academic hub.

Another way is to establish our own version of the Peace Corps. This will provide opportunities for young Singaporeans to work in other developing countries for short periods of time.

Ultimately, we aspire to be a society that is open and open-minded, thinking and acting as part of the world community of nations; and while our work, leisure, circumstances or yearnings may take us to the far corners of the world, we hope always to remain Singaporean in our hearts and in our minds.

Heng Choon Boon on Operation Raleigh in Panama. During his three-month stint, he helped build a hut for a villager suffering from muscular dystrophy, assisted in a reptile survey and trekked across Panama.

SUKA

NEWS

Singapore United Kingdom Association

On a chilly Sunday afternoon in October 1988, 60 people gathered at the Singapore High Commission in London. They were there to attend the inaugural meeting of SUKA, the Singapore (UK) Association, and to enrol as founder members.

SUKA was born out of the desire of Singaporeans, ex-Singaporeans and friends of Singapore living and working in Britain to get together from time to time, in the spirit of a community bound by their ties to Singapore.

Just weeks later, SUKA News, a bi-monthly newsletter, was launched. It not only carries news from Singapore, but is also a symbol of the strong and united Singapore spirit in the UK, and of an unabashed Singaporean identity.

A self-funding, non-political association, SUKA has become a vibrant rallying point for Singaporeans living in the United Kingdom. It organizes social, cultural, recreational and educational activities. The 350 SUKA members get together for family outings, to celebrate Singapore's National Day and other festivals, and to enjoy Singapore food. They celebrated the 25th Anniversary with gusto and panache, holding a Singapore tiffin reception at a posh London club, and despatching a delegation home to join in the celebrations.

SUKA offers its members a sense of fellowship and the feeling of warmth, care and camaraderie of a truly Singaporean community. It is an example of how we can help Singapore families abroad keep their links with Singapore.

National Security

All our hopes for the future depend on continuing national security. This is a fundamental requirement. National security means not just defending our sovereignty and territory but protecting our trade links and our right to live and prosper.

The Problem of Small States

Small states are like small fish. A small fish lives in an uncertain environment, where danger from bigger fish is a constant factor in its existence. Undercurrents can suddenly suck a small fish into more dangerous waters. To survive, a small fish requires vigilance and ingenuity.

Singapore is a small fish. Our land area of 626 square kilometres is by far the smallest in the region. We have a small population of just under 2.7 million and no natural resources. Located at the southern end of the Malacca Straits, our strategic importance is obvious. Here air and sea links intersect. Here lie the gateways to the Indian and Pacific Oceans. Demographically, we are multiracial with ethnic ties to countries inside and outside the region. Economically, Singapore's lack of natural resources forces us to rely on world trade. Survival means keeping our air, land and sea links open at all times.

The Region

Our region has a history of turbulence and conflict. Long ago, the ancient rival expanding empires of Majapahit and Siam attacked Temasek (old Singapore), then a wealthy trading city of Srivijaya. For centuries, the Portuguese, Dutch and English fought for influence here. We suffered Japanese occupation during the Second World War and watched the Vietnam War with anxiety.

The period immediately before and after Singapore's independence was one of uncertainty as countries in the region came to terms with one another's national aspirations. There were many disputes and misunderstandings. But we managed to resolve our differences. Outside Indochina, regional stability facilitated economic growth. This relatively

Our future depends on our taking responsibility to uphold and protect the sovereignty of our nation.

"All our hopes for the future depend on continuing national security."

" It [Vietnam's invasion of Cambodia in 1978] was a rude reminder ... never to take regional security for granted."

The first FPDA land exercise, Lion Spirit '89, held in Singapore.

Below and opposite: Bilateral army exercises, Semangat Bersatu and Safkar Indopura, jointly held with Malaysia and Indonesia respectively in 1989.

peaceful period was, however, shattered when Vietnam invaded its much smaller neighbour Cambodia in 1978 and occupied it for more than 11 years. It was a rude reminder to us never to take regional stability for granted.

Strategies for National Security

Small states can adopt several strategies to reduce their vulnerability. A fish swimming in a shoal is in less danger of being singled out for attack by larger fish. Singapore "swims" in several "shoals" for greater security. The first shoal is the Five Powers Defence Arrangements (FPDA) comprising the United Kingdom, Australia, New Zealand, Malaysia and Singapore. This shoal reinforces the security of both Malaysia and Singapore. The second shoal is ASEAN. ASEAN solidarity deters aggression from powers outside the region. The third shoal is the United Nations, which plays an increasingly important role in the preservation of world peace and order.

"ASEAN solidarity deters aggression from powers outside the region."

Singapore has long supported the maintenance of regional stability through a balance of power in the region. Over the last 40 years, the presence of the US has discouraged other powers from destabilizing the region. The US is a friendly big fish whose presence deters other big fish from adventure. A sudden US withdrawal would cause uncertainty and encourage others to fill the vacuum. This is why we support the US military presence. This is why Singapore has offered the US increased use of its military facilities.

Total Defence

Ultimately, however, a small state must be prepared to fight and defend itself. Alliances and diplomacy are helpful but they do not guarantee our security. In the marine world some fish are equipped with ingenious devices to ward off predators. The puffer fish, for example, will bloat itself up to look bigger and more menacing than it really is to frighten off assailants. It is poisonous as well. The stone fish, also highly poisonous, pretends to be a rock so that predators do not notice it. But it is unlikely

"Ultimately … a small state must be prepared to fight and defend itself."

that a strategically-located small state can merge with its surroundings and be overlooked. We should be like the poison shrimp with bright colours to warn others of the poison we carry.

Singapore has adopted a policy of Total Defence. Its objective is national resilience. Total Defence strengthens our overall defence capability against external aggression. It also promotes social cohesion, minimizing internal threats to our security.

An important component of Total Defence is the Singapore Armed Forces (SAF). Should war threaten, the SAF becomes crucial. National servicemen and reservists who make up our defence forces are fundamental to our security. They make many personal sacrifices to keep the armed forces in a high state of readiness. It is only fair that society recognizes their vital contribution, and ensures that they do not lose out compared to other Singaporeans.

"The objective of Total Defence is national resilience."

Every Singaporean participates in Total Defence in one capacity or another. Left: Reservists reporting back in an open mobilization exercise.

Below: Civil resource owners make available their vehicles during a civil resource mobilization exercise.

Civil defence volunteers and residents participate in an emergency water-rationing exercise(left) and in an MRT bomb shelter exercise(below).

The Future

A small fish is not defenceless. It can seek security in numbers; it can develop its own defences against predators. This in essence is Singapore's national security strategy to safeguard our inheritance and our future.

But we must also swim with the flow of world currents. The prospects for regional stability and prosperity have improved. With the end of the Cold War, we can expect a general relaxation of world tension, provided Iraq does not get away with its conquest of Kuwait. As the security environment becomes more favourable, we should adapt and adjust our policies. Of course we must always beware of sudden undertows in the region. But if we remain vigilant and keep our guard up, we can swim more confidently into the future.

"... if we remain vigilant and keep our guard up, we can swim more confidently into the future."

Racial and religious harmony is an important element of Singapore's social defence.

The Next Lap...

"The final contribution the old guard can make is to hand over to a younger team capable of ensuring continuing good government. We have exercised power as trustees of the people, always mindful of our fiduciary responsibility. Our sense of duty to our people made us exercise power honestly and scrupulously.

Singapore's future stability and progress depend on Goh Chok Tong's team having this same sense that they are trustees, conscious that if they abuse the power that they are entrusted with, they will betray the people who have to depend on them."

Lee Kuan Yew
at National Day Rally Speech in Mandarin
on August 26, 1990

"The torch has passed from one generation of runners to the next. But the race continues. I will use the collective talents of my colleagues, and the combined energies of all citizens, to help the Singapore team stay ahead.

Singapore can do well only if her good sons and daughters are prepared to dedicate themselves to help others. I shall rally them to serve the country. For if they do not come forward, what future will we have? I therefore call on my fellow citizens to join me, to run the next lap together."

Goh Chok Tong
at swearing-in ceremony on November 28, 1990

"The idealism, imagination and hope of youth are essential preconditions to create a better future."

Acknowledgements

We try to acknowledge by name below all those who have contributed directly or indirectly to the production of this book, in particular, those who sat as members of committees and task forces. But we will have left out some names inadvertently for which we apologise.

LONG TERM NATIONAL DEVELOPMENT COMMITTEE (1989-90)

Chairman: George Yeo, Members: Yeo Cheow Tong, Tay Eng Soon, Lee Boon Yang, Peter Sung, Mah Bow Tan, Seet Ai Mee, Ngiam Tong Dow, Secretariat: Low Sin Leng, Paul Cheung

Sub-Committee on Long Term Population Size
Chairman: Yeo Cheow Tong, Members: Teh Kok Peng, Toh Mun Heng, Koh Boon Hwee, Steven Goh, Teo Chee Hean, Tharman Shanmugaratnam, Charlotte Ng, Khoo Seok Lin, Paul Cheung

Sub-Committee on Long Term Education
Chairman: Seet Ai Mee, Members: Tan Cheng Bock, Goh Choon Kang, Lim Hock, Lim Jit Poh, Yeo Seng Teck, Eliza Quek, Zainul Abidin Rasheed, Leo Tan, Koh Boon Hwee, Ho Kwon Ping, Sulojana Natarajan, Mohammad Alami Musa, Secretariat: Peter Kwang

Sub-Committee on the Lowest Socio-Economic Group in Singapore
Chairman: Tay Eng Soon, Members: S Vasoo, Zulkifli bin Mohammed, Aline Wong, Nasser Kamaruddin, Matthias Yao, Lim Hsiu Mei, Paul Cheung, Secretariat: Indra Chelliah

Sub-Committee on Land Use and Quality of Life
Chairman: Lee Boon Yang, Members: Max Le Blond, Kenneth Chen, Alan Choe, Lee Phui Mun, Joseph McNally, Tisa Ng, Sim Wong Kooi, Tan Eng Liang, Tay Kheng Soon, Aline Wong, Ngiam Tong Dow, Liu Thai Ker, Lim Hng Kiang, Wang Mong Lin, Raymond Toh, John Keung, Zukiflee bin Moh Zaki, Secretariat: Cheong Koon Hean

Steering Committee on International Planning and Transportation Conference
Chairman: Lim Hng Kiang, Members: Ong Kok Min, Wang Mong Lin, Pok Sheung Foo, Khoo Teng Chye, Chua Koon Hoe, Yang Ai Fong, Secretariat: Cheong Koon Hean

Steering Committee for Overseas Singapore Clubs
Chairman: Peter Sung, Co-Chairman: George Yeo, Members: S Chandra Das, Andrew Chew, Peter Chan, Er Kwong Wah, Philip Yeo, Yeo Seng Teck, Cheong Choong Kong, P Y Hwang, Patrick Yeoh, Lim Swee Say, Wong-Lee Siok Tin, Evelyn Sen, Charlotte Ng, Secretariat: Low Choon Ming, Teo Kah Beng

Contributors
Ahmad Mattar, Chan Heng Chee, Chan Soo Sen, Chang Shuh Ling, Cheong Quee Wah, Andrew Chew, Chew Tai Soo, Chia Mia Chiang, Barry Desker, S Dhanabalan, Bee Wan Ditzig, Ee Peng Liang, Er Kwong Wah, Andress Goh, Goh Chin Tong, Goh Chok Tong, Goh Kim Leong, Peter Ho, Hsu Tze-Kwang, Richard Hu, S Jayakumar, John Keung, Khoo Chian Kim, Khoo Chin Hean, Koh Cher Siang, Koh Eng Kheng, Michael Koh, Koh Siong Ling, Tommy Koh, Koh Yong Guan, Kwa Soon Bee, Lam Chuan Leong, Lee Ek Tieng, Lee Hsien Loong, Lee Kuan Yew, Lee Mun Hou, Lee Poh Keng, Lee Yock Suan, Lim Sah Soon, Lim Siong Guan, Kishore Mahbubani, Moh Siew Meng, Jeya Mohideen, K N Nathan, Charlotte Ng, Ong Teng Cheong, Ong Wee Hock, J Y Pillay, See Chak Mun, Sharon Siddique, Soon Tuan Tee, Tan Chin Nam, Tan Chin Tiong, Tan Guong Ching, Tan See Nin, Tony Tan Keng Yam, Tay Kheng Soon, Simon Tay, Thung Syn Neo, K V Veloo, Aline Wong, Wong Hung Khim, Wong Kai Yeng, Wong Kan Seng, Yeo Ning Hong, Vincent Yip, Zaid bin Hamzah

Editorial Committee and Chapter Contributors
Low Sin Leng, Paul Cheung, Pek Siok Ching, Jaspal Singh, Ismail Sudderuddin, Teo Hee Lian, Carol Liew, Han Fook Kwang, Gretchen Liu, Cheong Koon Hean, Simon de Cruz, Foo Meng Liang, Peter Kwang, Lee How Sheng, Lee Yoke Kwang, Lim Hsiu Mei, Daniel Selvaretnam, Beatrice Tay

COMMITTEE FOR "BUILDING A FIRM FOUNDATION" (1990)

Kan Sou Tin, Mary Gomez, Loo Cheng Peng, Mrs Hardip Singh, Jumaat Masdawood, Rosalind Heng, Fong Yuet Kwai, Anthony Tan, Hwang-Lee P S, Tan Yock Leng, Ada Ponnappa, Dominic Yip, Wong Sin Eng, Foo Soo Luang, Anna Tham, Ho Chin Geok, Ting Beng Chin, Nanda Bandara, Chen Keng Juan, Lim Keng Boon, Joseph Lim, Nicholas Tang

NATIONAL INSTITUTE OF EDUCATION PLANNING COMMITTEE (1990)

Chairman: Seet Ai Mee, Members: Huang Hsing Hua, Dixie Tan, Bernard Tan, Ernest Chew, Sim Wong Kooi, Paul D Robinson, Er Kwong Wah, John Yip Soon Kwong, Lee Phui Mun, Foo Chee Meng, Peter Kwang, Charlotte Beck

COMMITTEE FOR "NANYANG TECHNOLOGICAL UNIVERSITY: FUTURE DIRECTIONS" (1990)

Michael Fam, Yeo Seng Teck, Cham Tao Soon, Chen Charng Ning, Alan Choe, Philip Pillai, Ling Sing Wong, Pek Beng Choon

COMMITTEE ON PRIMARY SCHOOL STREAMING & VOCATIONAL EDUCATION RESTRUCTURING (1990)

John Yip Soon Kwong, Law Song Seng, Lin Cheng Tong, Robert Chua, Horst Dunsche, N Varaprasad, Wee Heng Tin, Tan Yap Kwang, Wilson Lim, Tan Tiek Kwee, Yeow Chien Chien, Peter Kwang

AUTOMATION MANPOWER DEVELOPMENT COMMITTEE (1990)

Chairman: Leung Shiu Kee, Members: Andrew Nee, Lennie Lim, Quah Kok Wah, Tan Ah Sway, Cheong Sun Sin, Boo Kheng Hua, Richard Kwok, G H Tan, T Shida, James Teo, Goh Chin Kee, Chew Whye

AUTOMATION INFRASTRUCTURE DEVELOPMENT WORKING COMMITTEE (1990)

Chairman: Liew Mun Leong, Members: James Ling, Ho Nai Choon, Lothar Berghoff, Hoong Cheong Onn, Pang Siong Fatt, Victor Ho, Peter Boo, Ong Geok Soo, Tan Pui Guan, Boo Kheng Hua,

Acknowledgements

Wong Kok Seng, Linda Sein, Lye Weng Fong, Andrew Nee, Chan Siew Poh, Secretariat: James Ng

STUDY TEAM ON THE BUSINESS PARK (1990)
Chairman: Tan Lien Seng, Members: John Keung, Tan See Nin, Zulkifli Mohd, Han Yong Hoe, Lim Soo Chin, Chang Kwang Seh, Seah Kee Pok, Wong Kok Seng, Yap Mong Lin, Ong Yuet Fah

SUBMISSIONS ON SHARED VALUES (1990)
Joseph McNally, Pasir Panjang Indian Muslim Association, KGMS, NUS Political Science Society, AWARE, Junior Pyramid, Singapore Federation of Chinese Clan Associations, Junior College Students, Joint (Ad-hoc) Committee of Muslim Organisations, Gifted Children, J S Bandal, Tamil Representative Council, Taman Bacaan, Baha'i Faith, IPS Study Group, Jon S T Quah, Chiew Seen Kong, Leo Suryadinata, Zainul Abidin Rasheed, Arun Mahizhnan

INSTITUTE FOR AUTOMATION TECHNOLOGY STUDY GROUP (1989)
Chairman: Andrew Nee, Members: Ho Nai Choon, David Haines, Lew Ching Yoong, Danny Lam, Ng Chee Kiong, Tan Hong San, Secretariat: Manohar Khiatani

AUTOMATION CULTURE DEVELOPMENT COMMITTEE (1989)
Chairman: Leo Tan, Members: Patrick Daniel, Seng Han Thong, Pang Tong Hup, Chew Whye, Param Ajeet Singh Bal, Wong Kok Siew, Ow Chin Cheow, Catherine Chua, Secretariat: Manohar Khiatani

NATIONAL MARKETING WORKSHOP (NMW) COMMITTEES (1989)
NMW Work Group On Product (Infrastructure)
Co-Chairmen: Tan Guong Ching, Ng Kiat Chong, Lim Ho Kee, Members: Ang Swee Tian, Albert Hong, Cheng Wai Keung, Dennis Brown, Francis Mak, Jen Shek Voon, John Keung, Koh Beng Seng, Lee Chee Yeng, Lee Loong Koon, Lee Yong Siang, Leong Cheng Chit, Lim Hng Kiang, Lim Hock San, Ong Kok Min, Sung Sio Ma, Tan Puay Chiang, Tan Swan Beng, William O'Shea, Wong Chun Win, Wong Hoi Kit, Wong Seng Hon, Secretariat: Gan Chong Ger, Wong Hong Wai

NMW Work Group On Product (Capabilities)
Co-Chairmen: Er Kwong Wah, Leong Chee Whye, Lim Pin, Members: Cham Tao Soon, Charlotte Ng, Chen Hung, Chris Tan Y H, Hsieh Fu Hua, Ian C Buchanan, John Yip, Johnny Moo, Khoo Kay Chai, Koh Juan Kiat, Law Song Seng, Lee Miew Boey, Liew Mun Leong, Lim Siam Kim, Lin Cheng Ton, Ng Pock Too, Ronald Ho, Tang Siu Shing, Victor Lye, Vincent Yip, Wong Lin Hong, Yeo Khee Leng, Secretariat: Lee Soon Khuan, Valerie Lim

NMW Work Group On Product (Environment)
Co-Chairmen: Cheong Quee Wah, Liu Thai Ker, Ang Kong Hua, Members: Chen Ai Ju, Chua Sian Eng, Elizabeth Tan, Goh Hup Chor, How Peck Huat, Kenneth Chen, Lai Choon Seng, Lau Teng Chuan, Lau Woh Cheong, Ng Yew Kang, Pamelia Lee, Rafiq Jumabhoy, Robert Chua, Tan Gee Paw, Tan Lien Seng, Tan See Lai, Tony Irons, Wee Eng Lim, Secretariat: Ng Nam Sin, Elaine Teo

NMW Work Group On Price
Co-Chairmen: Moh Siew Meng, Yeo Seng Teck, Ho Kwon Ping, Members: Ajith Prasad, Barry Lennon, Chia Choon Wei, Daniel Selvaretnam, Goh Tiak Theng, John Hubby, Michael Yeo, Ng Chee Keong, Chang Kwang Seh, Ng Keat Seng, Ng Wee Hiong, Peter Connell, Swee Kee Siong, Tan Bock Seng, Tharman Shanmugaratnam, Secretariat: Sonny Tan, Linda Sein

NMW Work Group On Place/ Promotion/Power
Co-Chairmen: Lam Chuan Leong, John Wong, Tan Chin Nam, Members: Andrew Sng, Billy Lee, Chew Tai Soo, Chia Shi Teck, David Chin, Fock Siew Wah, Evelyn Sen, Koh Boon Hwee, Lai Seck Khui, Lim Swee Say, Lim Toon, Ng Kok Song, Peter Ho, Philip Pillai, Rick Foxhoven, Roy M Barbee, Sonnie Lien, Takao Yuhara, Secretariat: Liu Shih Shin, Ow Chin Cheow, John Lok

NMW Work Group On Public Relations
Co-Chairmen: Peter Chan, Goh Kim Leong, Wong Nang Jang, Members: Jonathan Blum, David J Browning, Chan Heng Wing, Chee Lay Hong, Bob Chew, W F Driese, Foo Meng Tong, James Fu, S K Gan, Rick Harrison, Ko Kheng Hwa, C K Lee, Lee Cheow Seng, Lee Ying Cheun, Leong Wai Leng, Low Sin Leng, Kishore Mahbubani, Arun Mahizhnan, Kazuo Mihara, Matthew Samuel, V Somogy, Teo Ming Kian, Wong-Lee Siok Tin, Secretariat: Ong Choon Hwa, Thong Pao Yi, Susan Wang, Anne Koh, Alan Tan, Veronica Lim

COMMITTEE FOR THIRD POLYTECHNIC (1989)
Chairman: Tay Eng Soon, Members: Er Kwong Wah, John Yip Soon Kwong

Third Polytechnic Working Group
N Varaprasad, Chan Chee Wah, Cheng Huang Leng, F A Vasenwala, Lin Cheng Ton, Lye Hoeng Fai, Moses Yu, Ng Kee Choe, Pakir Singh, Roselin Liew Yin Wah, Tan Yap Kwang, Young Pak Nang, Lee Keow Jit

ADVISORY COUNCIL ON YOUTH (1989)
Chairman: Lee Hsien Loong, Deputy Chairman: Abdullah Tarmugi, Members: Goh Song How, Ling Diong Hee, Geraldine Li-Ming Loh, Ho Kong Chong, Dick Lee, Lim Tat, Mohd Yusoff Marican, Nasser Kamaruddin, Ng Han Seong, Irene Pates, Kenneth Tan Khoon Tuan, David Wong Wei Li, Yong Pow Ang, Secretariat: Tan Kin Hian, Tan Kia Jin, Khoo Saik Chin, Gwee Swee Geok, Goh Chim Khim

Committee on Students and Early School Leavers
Chairman: Geraldine Li-Ming Loh, Co-Chairman: Ho Kong Chong, Members: Yong Pow Ang, Irene Pates, Irene Yong Swee Lan, Secretariat: How Bee Lan, Ho Joo Seok

Committee on Pre-Working and Working Youths
Chairman: Goh Song How, Members: Lim Tat, Dick Lee, Edward Leong Chee Keen, Kenneth Tan Khoon Tuan, Ravindran s/o Ramasamy, Jason Lau Wei Terk, Quek Hung Tong, Secretariat: Joyce Chia Yoke Funn, Lee Peck Siam

Committee on Young Adults
Chairman: Ling Diong Hee, Members: Mohd Yusoff Marican, Nasser Kamaruddin,

Acknowledgements

Ng Han Seong, David Wong Wei Li, Chim Hou Yan, Lee Chong Kai, Emily Choi Yok Hung, Secretariat: Yee Boon Ling, Goh Siew Yem

ADVISORY COUNCIL ON SPORT AND RECREATION (1989)
Chairman: S Dhanabalan, Members: C J Chen, Edward D' Silva, Er Kwong Wah, Edward Jacob, Lee Chiong Giam, Lim Neo Chian, Paul D Robinson, Seah Lye Huat, Tan Eng Liang, Tan Hock Lye, Dennis Tay, Othman Wok, Secretariat: Lau Teng Chuan

Contributors
Cheng Tuck Siung, Chong Poo Aik, Hoo Yew Gee, Juwahri bin Sarip, Kenny Khoo Cheng Swee, Lee Kim Tah, Kevin Leong, S Manevasan, N Mohan, Raffles Institution (192 submissions from students), S T Ratnam, Tan Kee Ngah, Daniel Wee Wun Ming, Archery Association of Singapore, Australian Sports Marketing Pte Ltd, Bartley Secondary School, Changi Sailing Club, Kim Keat Community Centre Management Committee, Ngee Ann Polytechnic, Outram Institute, People's Action Party Suburban Central District, Raffles Junior College, Singapore Amateur Athletic Association, Singapore Amateur Gymnastics Association, Singapore Chess Federation, Singapore Chinese Chamber of Commerce & Industry, Singapore General Hospital, Singapore Lawn Tennis Association, Singapore Polytechnic, Singapore Polytechnic Academic Staff Association, Singapore Rifle Association, Singapore Sea Sports Liaison Committee, Singapore Squash Rackets Association, Singapore Table Tennis Association, Singapore Water Ski Federation,

Singapore Women's Hockey Association, Singapore Yachting Association, Thomson Community Centre Management Committee, Tung Ann District Guild, Volleyball Association of Singapore

ADVISORY COUNCIL ON FAMILY AND COMMUNITY LIFE (1989)
Chairman: Wong Kan Seng, Members: Chong Kim Chang, Chow Kok Fong, Koh Cher Siang, Kwa Chong Bee, Lee Chiong Giam, Ngiam Tee Liang, Peter G H Owyong, Peh Chin Hua, N Subramaniam, S Vasoo, Aline Wong, Yahya Aljaru, Secretariat: Lim Sah Soon, Mrs Lim Eng Seng, Lee Yuen Hee, Indra Chelliah, Ang Bee Lian

Contributors
Grace Chen, Chong Poo Aik, Chua Lay Mee, Veronica Jayeram, Irving Lazar, Lee Kim Tah, Leong Wai Kum, A K Markandu, T S Nathen, Irene Pates, Vivien Tan

Committee on Family Life
Chairman: Ngiam Tee Liang, Members: Lam Sian Lian, Lee Sze Leong, Lim Hsiu Mei, J K Medora, Peh Chin Hua, Pek Beng Choon, Peter G H Owyong, Siti Hamidah bte Abdullah Bahashwan, Tan Seow Peer, Thung Syn Neo, Wong Sze Tai, Yahya Aljaru, Anthony Yeo, Secretariat: Mrs Lim Eng Seng, Ang Bee Lian, Gilbert Fan, Doreen Loh

Committee on Community Life
Chairman: Aline Wong, Co-Chairman: Khoo Boon Hui, Members: Charlotte Beck, Chow Kok Fong, Chua Beng Huat, Goh Tiam Lock, Heng Chee How, Henry Lim, Lim Sah Soon, Eric Low, Mitherpal Singh, Mohd Daing Farhan bin Hashim, Jeffrey Po Gim Tee, N

Subramaniam, Tham Yew Fang, Wong Chin Tiang, Secretariat: Lee Yuen Hee, Ang Bee Lian

Committee on Destitute Families
Chairman: S Vasoo, Members: Mrs Jaya Anand, Cyril Chew, Chong Kim Chang, Koh Gee Kum, Lim Hsiu Mei, Mrs Lim Eng Seng, Lim Ewe Huat, Lim Koon Heng, Siti Hamidah bte Abdullah Bahashwan, Teo Lye Huat, Wong Chin Yeow, Yow Kwok Sum, Secretariat: Indra Chelliah, Ng Bie Hah, Mrs Ismail Ellias, Laurence Wee, Mrs Lim Liang Ching

ADVISORY COUNCIL ON CULTURE AND THE ARTS (1989)
Chairman: Ong Teng Cheong, Members: Koh Cher Siang, Er Kwong Wah, Robert Iau, Tay Kheng Soon, Edwin Thumboo, Yeo Seng Teck, Arun Mahizhnan, Wong-Lee Siok Tin, Loy Teck Juan, Leslie Fong, Suhaimi Jais, Hawazi bin Daipi, Ho Kwon Ping, Vincent Yip, Chia Kee Koon, Secretariat: Ng Yew Kang, Juliana Chua

Committee on Heritage
Chairman: Tay Kheng Soon, Members: Foo Meng Liang, Lee Wai Kok, Leow Jwee How, Ernest Chew, P Selvadurai, Jeffrey Chan, Rafiq Jumabhoy, Gwee Yee Hean, Mansor Adabi, David Lim, Lee Kip Lin, Tan Kim Siew, Secretariat: Kwa Chong Guan, Daniel Chew

Contributors
Lim Hng Kiang, Khoo Teng Chye, Ho Cheok Sun, Wen Kai Meng, Leong Chee Chiew, Goh Hup Chor, Koh-Lim Wen Gin, Low Chwee Lye, Lee Sing Kong, Tan Wee Kiat, Andrew Cheng, N Namazie, Zaleha Tamby, Lily Tan, Hedwig Anuar, Lim Kek Hwa, David Chng, Lin Wo Ling, Vivien

Wee, Chan Heng Chee, Francis Wong, C K Leong, Alvin Lim, Tan Geok Koon, Chong Poo Aik, Gwee Thian Hock, Lee Guan Kai, Pang Hui Siang, Heng Chiang Meng, William Lim, Sharon Siddique, Ilsa Sharp, Wong Yew Kwan

Working Group on Fine Arts Heritage
Chairman: Tay Kheng Soon, Members: Kwa Chong Guan, Daniel Chew, Constance Sheares, T K Sabapathy, Irene Lim, Chan Heng Wing

Working Group on Heritage of the Man-Made Environment and the Natural Environment
Chairman: Rafiq Jumabhoy, Members: David Lim, Lee Kip Lin, Tay Kheng Soon, Tan Kim Siew

Working Group on Documentary Records
Chairman: Ernest Chew, Members: Kwa Chong Guan, Daniel Chew

Working Group on Lifestyles, Traditions and Institutions
Chairman: Jeffrey Chan, Members: Mansor Adabi, Leow Jwee How, Gwee Yee Hean, P Selvadurai

National Heritage Trust Task Force
Chairman: Jeffrey Chan, Members: Tay Kheng Soon, P Selvadurai, Mansor Adabi, Lee Wai Kok, Rafiq Jumabhoy, Leow Jwee How, Ernest Chew, Kwa Chong Guan, Daniel Chew

Committee on Literary Arts
Chairman: Edwin Thumboo, Members: Foo Meng Liang, Lee Wai Kok, Robert Yeo, Lee Tzu Pheng, Wong Yoon Wah, Mohd Naim B Daipi, V T Arasu, K Elanggovan, Matthias Yao, Secretariat: Lee Fei Chen, Chiam Peak Yuen

Acknowledgements

Contributors
National Book Council of Pakistan, Embassy of the Federal Republic of Germany, Royal Norwegian Embassy, Malaysian High Commission, Swedish Embassy, Embassy of Japan, Royal Thai Embassy, Australian High Commission, Royal Danish Embassy, Embassy of Israel, British Council, New Zealand High Commission, Embassy of the Republic of Korea, Kumpulan Angkatan Muda Sastera, Abdul Samad bin Salimin, Razif Hj Bahari, Sharifah Maznah Syed Omar, M K Narayanan, P Krishnan, Rama Kannabiran, Pandian R, M S Sanmugam, Muthu Manikam, A P Shanmugam, Seve Shanmugam, Tan Suan Chyang, Lau Wai Har, Cheng Kin Pak, Chong Fun Liam, Hsing Chi Chung, Liaw Yock Fang, Leo Suryadinata, Chia Hwee Pheng, Liaw Yock Eng, Philip Jeyaretnam, Ho Minfong, Daniel Koh, Ho Poh Fun, Goh Sin Tub, Lim Li, Heng Siok Tian, Edward Phua, Felix Cheong, Woo Keng Thye, Lim Thean Soo, National University of Singapore, Institute of Education, Vocational and Industrial Training Board, Ngee Ann Polytechnic, Language Proficiency Centre, Berita Harian/Berita Minggu, The Straits Times, Shin Min Daily News, Lianhe Zaobao/Lianhe Wanbao, Hong Leong Foundation, The Loke Cheng-Kim Foundation, Tan Kah Kee Foundation, Japanese Chamber of Commerce and Industry of Singapore, Singapore Federation of Chambers of Commerce & Industry, Singapore International Chamber of Commerce, Singapore Indian Chamber of Commerce, Nestle Singapore, Singapore Offshore Petroleum Services Pte Ltd, BP Singapore Pte Ltd, Mobil Oil Singapore Pte Ltd, United Overseas Bank, Overseas Union Bank, Development Bank of Singapore, Shell Companies in Singapore, Esso Singapore Pte Ltd, V J Times, Ministry of Education – Curriculum Planning Division & Curriculum Development Institute of Singapore, Singapore Indian Artistes Association, Sadasivam Veriyah, Koh Tai Ann, Michael Wee, Lee Song Mun, Chong Poo Aik, Goh Swee Tee

Sub-Committee on the Promotion of Reading
Chairman: Lee Tzu Pheng, Members: Anne Pakir, Paul Jansen, Mavis Siregar, Loo Yin Hong, N Govindasamy, Fauziah Soeratman, Marie Bong, Vasantha Kumaree Siva, Secretariat: Chiam Peak Yuen

Committee on Performing Arts
Chairman: Robert Iau, Members: Foo Meng Liang, Lee Wai Kok, Bernard Tan, Phoon Yew Tien, Georgina Emmanuel, Joseph Peters, Sydney Tan, Radhika Srinivasan, Max Le Blond, Lam Pin Foo, Nadiputra, Kuo Pao Kun, S Varathan, Tan It Koon, Lim Fei Shen, Uma Rajan, Cecilia Hon, Som Said, Ahmad Jaffar, Secretariat: Goh Ching Lee, Valerie Lim, Irene Wong, Maureen Teo

Contributors
Wong-Lee Siok Tin, Param Singh, Chandra Mohan, Ananda Perera, Sebastian Tan, Loong May Lin, Chua Foo Yong, Andrew Cheng, Sandra Buenaventura, Ung Gim Sei, Foo Ket, Pan Zhenlei, Lin Fengying, Lin Chunlan, Huang Yuyun, Tan Chang Meng, Han Sanyuan, Goh Nguen Wah, Tay Boon Hui, Foong Choon Hon, Paul Ning, Goh Lee Eng, Lim Quee Heok, Lee Chee Ngai, Chua Gim Siong, Lim Kuan Kang, Teo Han Eng, Toh Teck Guan, Ser Cheng Chuan, Teng Yu Er, Soo Geok Keen, Gan Beng Lee, Tan Teck Hui, Low Siew Eng, Lee Ghee Kiong, Lim Choon Siew, D Natarajan, A Sachithananthan, Shashilal Kashyap, V Vigneswaran, N Subramaniam, A N Rao, M Bala Subramanion, S Sribaran, Arun Mahizhnan, I S Menon, Roger Jenkins, S Varathan, K P Bhaskar, Abdullah Shafie bin Mohd Sidik, Chua Soo Pong, Leslie Wong, Koh Chong Chiah, Yeo Koh Phew, Singapore Federation of Chinese Clans, Principal, Outram Secondary School, Cheng Tuck Siung, Tan Geok Koon, Vice-Principal, Bartley Secondary School, Maha Sripathy, Constance Singam, Vanitha Saravanan, Lee Song Mun, C K Leong, Su Kee Lay, Yee Fook Hong, Philip Chin, Sadasivam Veriyah, Lee Guan Kai, Lew Mi Fon, Shane Thio, Chong Poo Aik, Wong S W David, Teh Yap Cheng, Principal, Clementi North Primary School, Chew Yong Soo, Chan Fook Pong, Heng Chiang Meng, Toh Joo Hock

Sub-Committee on Dance
Chairman: Tan It Koon, Members: Lim Fei Shen, Uma Rajan, Cecilia Hon, Som Said

Contributors
Goh Soo Khim, Anthony Then, Chua Soo Pong, Goh Lay Kuan, Rosalind Soo-Ho, Chia Meng Tze, Lim Fei Shen, Norenshah Sahari, Sharmini Jacob, Antony Tay Kok Cheng, Tan Tian Soh, Yan Choong Lian, Angelia Liong, Tony Llacer, Shirley Johnson, Mary Lim, Chee Soo Chern, Lim Beng Soon, Madhavi K S, Neila Satyalingam, Yap Pau Eng, Nongchik Ghani, Mr & Mrs K P Bhaskar, Bill Calhoun, Rose Eberwein, Hun Chin Guan, Koh Joh Ting, Yeo Siew Muey, Chang Shang Lok, Tay Boon Kiang, Seow Yoke Beng, Goh Siew Geok, See Ming Lee, Tang Kwek Leong, Lau Geok Hua, Wang Li Hwei, Pun Hong Peng, Maswari, Zahrian Osman, Salleh Buang, Hew Yee Min

Sub-Committee on Drama
Chairman: Max Le Blond, Members: Lam Pin Foo, Almahdi Al-haj Ibrahim, Kuo Pao Kun, S Varathan

Contributors
Roger Jenkins, Ruby Lim-Yang, Tan Beng Luan, Liew Song Hwa, Tan Khar Luang, Lee Chye Ee, Tay Lee Huat, Charles Koh, David Chen, S S Sarma, Liew Min, Nongchik Ghani, Rajagopal, Suresh Menon, Sameer Sugwekar, Lee Yew Moon, Veronica Minjoot, Perry Awyong, Alan Watkins-Groves, Ruth Low, Elvira Holmberg, S T Shimi, Reynold J Buono, Harjit Kaur, Fong Choon Sam, David Quak, Andrew Watts, Michael Wilson, Rebecca Mok, Tng Hia Seng, Karen Ooi, V Govindarrasu, Lee Yin Lin, Raymond Ong, Robert Yeo, ACT 3 Theatrics Pte Ltd, Lim Thean Soo, V Ramachandran, Christina Sergeant, Stella Kon, Jamil Mohd Yunos

Sub-Committee on Music
Chairman: Bernard Tan, Members: Phoon Yew Tien, Georgina Emmanuel, Joseph Peters, Sydney Tan, Ahmad Jafaar, Radhika Srinivasan

Contributors
Paul Abisheganaden, Lu Sinclair, Tonni Wei, Robin Henderson, Stuart McIntosh, Christopher Daniels, Robert Luse, Nick Richardson, Chee Woon Yang, I S Menon, Ku Lap Man, Leow Siak Fah, Pravel Prantl, Chng Kai Jin, Peter Low, Lim Yau, Jay Soo,

Acknowledgements

Gordon Jansen, Dick Lee, Jacintha Abisheganaden, Anchant Chales, Mel Ferdinands, Jeremy Monteiro, Billy Koh, Terry Undag, Babes Conde, Chong Poh Heng, Lynn Lee, Kee Chee Chuan, Tan Kim Chen, Yew Hong Jen, Shen Ping Kwang, Wong Wee Kong, Koh Nam Seng, Suzanna Jade Teo, Isaac J Farid, Ken Lim, Goh Keng Leng, Quek Yong Siu, Leong Yoon Pin, Sadli Ali, Mark Chan, Tarn Teh Ting, Lim Quee Heok, Chong Wing Hong, David Lim, Soon John Kwang, Ng Siew Eng, Lee Howe, Koh Hung Meng, Lim Tow Seng, Tham Chaik Kong, Ng Teck Seng, Tan Kim Lian, Yeo Siew Wee, Lian Yoong Liang, Lin Ah Lek, Phang Thean Siong, Lee Ngoh Wah, Lee Hoon Piek, Lim Sin Yeo, W D Anthony, Natarajan, Mrs Bagyamurthi, Robert Godfrey, Linda Fang, Neecia Maria Majolly, Robert Leong

Committee on Visual Arts
Chairman: Yeo Seng Teck, Members: Foo Meng Liang, Lee Wai Kok, Joseph McNally, Earl Lu, Tang Liang Hong, T K Sabapathy, Tan Swie Hian, David Tay, Marjorie Chu, Teo Eng Seng, Chia Wai Hon, Iskandar Jalil, Khoo Chin Hean, Secretariat: Richard Poh, Liew Chin Choy

Contributors
S E Chua, Tan Siah Kwee, Chan Fook Fong, Katherine Ho, People's Action Party Suburban Central District

Working Group On New Cultural Development Agency
Chairman: Arun Mahizhnan, Members: Foo Meng Liang, Ng Yew Kang, Vincent Yip, Ho Kwon Ping, Hawazi bin Daipi, Secretariat: Juliana Chua

ADVISORY COUNCIL ON THE AGED (1989)
Chairman: S Jayakumar, Members: Chen Ai Ju, Ee Peng Liang, Gan Cheong Chor, F J Jayaratnam, Koh Cher Siang, Stephen Lee, Moh Siew Meng, Alan Ow Soon Sian, Hsuan Owyang, Shafawi bin Ahmad, Davinder Singh, Daniel Teo Tong How, Ann Wee, Secretariat: K V Veloo, Lee Wah Cheong, Janet Yee, Winnie Tang, Mok Pui Yim, Simon Sim Kay Yan, Chee Liee Chin, Koh Lay Tin

Contributors
Juliet McCully, Board of Visitors (Welfare Homes), Chee Kah Keng, S E Chua, Ee Peng Liang, C Fernandez, Goh Choon Seng, Joseph Ho Shun Fatt, T K K Iyer, Lee Kim Tah, Henry Lim, Annie Phoon, Phung Khye Sun, Principal, Woodlands Primary School, Rilly Ray, Fong Ngan-Phoon, R Kanaga Sabapathy, Seet Ai Mee, Besaka Singh, Ismail Talib, Tan Kee Ngah, Vice-Principal, Bartley Secondary School, Wat Chee Kok, Yap Kim Choy, Patrick Yap, Judy Yeok

Committee on Attitudes Towards the Aged
Chairman: Hsuan Owyang, Members: Robert P Balhetchet, Chen Yok Chin, Lim Hsiu Mei, Lee Wah Cheong, Davinder Singh, Wan Wah, Wu Teh Yao, Yeo Yek Seng, Sylvester Yong, Secretariat: Koh Lay Tin

Committee on Community-Based Programmes for the Aged
Chairman: Ann Wee, Members: Hasina bte Mohd Yusof, Kua Ee Heok, Li Shing, Benny Lim Siang Hoe, Lim Kok Eng, Lim Hsiu Mei, Lee Wah Cheong, Rilly Ray, Secretariat: Winnie Tang

Committee on Employment of the Aged
Chairman: Stephen Lee, Members: Lew Syn Pau, Lim Hoy Pick, Lim Hsiu Mei, Lee Wah Cheong, Albert Low Seng Chua, Low Wong Fook, Alan Ow Soon Sian, Tan Kin Lian, Secretariat: Mok Pui Yim

Committee on Residential Care Programmes for the Aged
Chairman: Ee Peng Liang, Members: Paul Cheung; Fong Ngan-Phoon, Khoo Teng Chye, Lim Chan Yong, Lim Hsiu Mei, Lee Wah Cheong, Sarojiuy Palakrishnan, Philip Tan Eng Seong, Daniel Teo Tong How, Secretariat: Janet Yee, Lee Wah Cheong

ADVISORY COUNCIL ON THE DISABLED (1988)
Chairman: Tony Tan Keng Yam, Deputy Chairman: Tay Eng Soon, Members: Kamal Bose, Chan Kai Yau, Chang Meng Teng, Maurice Choo, Er Kwong Wah, Koh Cher Siang, Koh Eng Kheng, Moh Siew Meng, Syed Haroon bin Mohamed Aljunied, Dixie Tan, Tan Guan Heng, Secretariat: K V Veloo, Lee Wah Cheong, Fok Fook Choon, Irene Kapoor, Koo Fai Lan, Lim Puay Tiak, Fok Yok Cheng

Contributors
Caroline de Souza, Dixie Tan, Poovana Thilakami, Jane Chang Hui Ten, Wong Kai Nam, Chan Mei Li, Kamal Bose, Patricia Lock, Roger Jenkins, HOPE Group, Robert Tan Jee Keng, Chong Wai Chuen, Gladys Ong Hong Hong, Patricia Yap, Joseph Ho Shun Fatt, Serene Lee, N Senevasan, Augustine Sam, Board of Visitors (Welfare Homes), Timothy Ang

Committee on Community Involvement and Residential Care for Disabled People
Chairman: Koh Eng Kheng, Members: S C Leonard, Lim Hsiu Mei, K V Veloo, Syed Haroon bin Mohamed Aljunied, Julie Tan, Teh Kong Leong, Richard Tong, Wong Tze Wai, Secretariat: Koo Fai Lan.

Working Group on Preventing Disability
Chairman: Maurice Choo, Members: Kamal Bose, Koh Eng Kheng, Kenneth Lyen, Dixie Tan, K V Veloo, Lim Puay Tiak

Committee on Education and Training of Disabled People
Chairman: Chan Kai Yau, Members: Kamal Bose, Chan Soo Sen, John Elliott, Fok Fook Choon, Lim Hsiu Mei, K V Veloo, Kenneth Lyen, Seet Ai Mee, Tan Hong Choon, Secretariat: Fok Fook Choon

Committee on Employment, Accessibility and Transportation for Disabled People
Chairman: Chang Meng Teng, Members: John Chan, Gerard Ee, Gan Kim Yong, Mike Gray, Lee Coo, Lim Hsiu Mei, K V Veloo, Lawrence Mah, Tan Guan Heng, Robert Yew, Secretariat: Irene Kapoor

NATIONAL AUTOMATION MASTER PLAN COMMITTEE (1988)
Chairman: Lai Chun Loong, Alternate Chairman: Tan Bock Seng, Members: Peter Boo, Rames C Chatterjee, Cheng Wai Keung, Gan Kim Song, Goh Chin Khee, Tomio Koide, Tsuneo Kunikata, Leong Cheng Chit, M LePleux, Patrick Lian, Johnny Lim, Lin Cheng Ton, James Ling, Andrew Nee, Ong Yen Her, Hal Price, Secretariat: Manohar Khiatani, Suresh Natarajan

Acknowledgements

INDUSTRY SUB-COMMITTEE OF THE NATIONAL LAND CONCEPT PLAN (1988)
Chairman: Leong Cheng Chit, Members: John Keung, Chang Yong Ching, Seetoh Kum Chun, Peter Tan, Lau Woh Cheong, Tam-Lai Seow Yoke, Han Fook Kwang, Leow Bee Geok, Tan Siong Leng, Khoo Chin Hean, Wong Seng Hon, Bong Kim Pin, Navaratne P A, Tan Yong Nang, Leong Peng Kiong, Judy Tan, Secretariat: Wong Kok Seng

SMALL AND MEDIUM ENTERPRISE WORKSHOP (SMEW) WORK GROUPS (1988)
SMEW *Work Group on Manufacturing Technology*
Chairman: Lai Chun Loong, Co-Chairman: Ong Phee Poh, Members: Peter Boo, Goh Yeow Tin, Thomas Koh, Padmini Krishnan, Ng Say Key, Su Kee Lay, Lee Ah Bee, Raymond Tay, Teng Beng Long, Lim Tock Yen, Jimmy Chew, Hwang Koh Chee, Yeo Khee Siang, Paul Binding, Lim Chiang Peng, Gawain Yan, Seow Poh Leok, Ricky K H Souw, Christopher Koh, Tan Khieng Sin, Benson Lin, Yong Choon, Jeremy Chong, David Leong, Foo Chee Chin, E H Lim, Ho Chung Lap, Lawrence Tay, Tan Sen Min, Ho Tsong Yueng, Alfred Tan, Lim Ee Ann, Chow Tat Kong, Lim Choon, Ooi Inn Bok, Timothy Sebastian, Resource Organisations: Brian Lee, Lennie Lim, Kam Booi Chung, Sajjad Akhtar, Lee Kok Foong, Poo Aun Neow, Secretariat: Heng Keng Wah, Leroy Lim, Chen Fui Lin

SMEW *Work Group on Business Development for Manufacturing*
Steering Committee
Chairman: Ho Kwon Ping, Co-Chairman: Foo Meng Tong, Members: John Chia, Tan Jee

Chin, Leslie Lim, Wong Chin Yeow, Wong Yean Seng, Chan Ven Lin, Cho Jock Min, Tony Lin, Regina Wong, Cheng Wai Keung, Low Sin Leng, Lim Hwee Guan, Lim Choon, Patrick Yang, John Lok, Lim Tow Cheng, Resource Organisations: Ning De Guzman, Goh Chung Meng, Secretariat: Jonathan Law

Work Group Members
Lim Aik Sun, William S K Ong, Edward Wong, Lim Chor Soon, Seck Hong Chee, P H Lim, Lim Lay Yew, Sunny Bay, Roger Low, Wee Kok Wah, Choo Ker Yong, Tan Geh, John Yeo, Michael Chan, Hon Shu, Tan Gek Suan, Matthew Tan

SMEW *Work Group on Technology for Commerce & Services*
Steering Committee
Chairman: Johnny Moo, Co-Chairman: Lim Swee Say, Members: Lin Jinn Sin, Robert Fu, George Abraham, Leong Chun Loong, Ong Siow Aik, John Lee, Chia Shi Teck, Ian Gan, Tang Wee Lip, Lee Fook Hong, David Chang, Florence Tay, Daniel Tan, David Hew, David Lim, George Lye, Lim Choon, Patrick Yang, Timothy Sebastian, Resource Organisation: David L Bushman, Teo Moh Gin, Sajjad A Akhtar, Secretariat: Yeo Khee Leng, Bob Chen

Work Group Members
Ko Kheng Hwa, Prem Kumar, Lee Eng Leun, Poh Yew Tay, Jeffrey Tan, Jamshid K Medora, Mohammed Nageb, Tan Tee Hwa, Wong Kum Sek, Soh Keng Wah, Ong Aik Boon, Jahari Hj Affandi, Chang Jin Aye, Wong Poi Kwong, Lee Bay Tseng, Lee Chin Chuan, Chan Wai Ming, Lam Wei Ying

SMEW *Work Group on Business Development for Commerce & Services*
Steering Committee
Chairman: Robert Iau, Co-Chairman: Tan Song Chuan, Members: Wang Ting Min, Eddie Chan, Adrian Teo, Earl Tan, Foo Der Rong, Monica Tomlin, Kwek Teng Swee, Tan Kah Hoe, Lee Lai Choo, Chionh Chye Khye, Daney Lim, Lim Choon, Patrick Yang, Seet Khai Yong, Resource Organisations: Tan Thiam Soon, R S Wickramasuriya, Subhash Mehta, Roger Poor, James Ho, Yang Thian Sze, Secretariat: Ko Khee Hwee, Thian Tai Chew, Matthew Sim

Work Group Members
Tan Lian Tong, Lee Fong Yuen, Abdul Kader Tyebally, Goh Kim Seng, Tan Beng Soon, Catherine Lim, Tang Chong Meng, Chua Song Peck, Howard Meitiner, Tan Poh Sik, Lim Fang Chee, Lee Kang Lam, Ong Huat Kee, Abdul Kadir

SMEW *Work Group on Productivity*
Steering Committee
Chairman: Bob Tan Beng Hai, Co-Chairman: Koh Juan Kiat, Members: Victor Ho, David Tong, Eunice Low, Mercy George, Lim Choon, Resource Organisations: W J Leininger, David Wong, Devan Janamitra, Secretariat: Chew Whye, Zainal Abidin, Tan Han Eng, Tan Koon Yee

Work Group Members
J K Gopalaratnam, Goh Nyang Kuang, Tan Chee Hong, S M Loh, Seow Poh Eng, Ong Sin Seng, Leonard Loo, Henry Goh, Eileen Tay, Choong Buat Ken, David Tan, Uttam P Kripalanl, Diong T P, Teo Tee Hua, Ng Ghit Chong, Leslie Ed, M J Bhojwani,

R Dhinakaran, Tan Aik Koon, Wong Bun Huge, Tan See Jong

SMEW *Work Group on Human Resource Management*
Steering Committee
Chairman: John Wong, Alt Chairman: Sunny Chan, Co-Chairman: Lyou Soon Tian, Members: Daron Liew, Soh Keng Wah, Paul Lim, Leow Siew Beng, Thian Boon Cheow, R Theyvandran, Lim Koon Heng, Lim Choon, Resource Organisations: Foo Tiang Sooi, Ma Kheng Min, Khoo Oon Theam, Lim Say Beng, Gan See Khem, Wee Beng Geok, F A Vasenwala, Tan Jin Hee, Cheng Huang Leng, Secretariat: Lee Soon Khuan, John Tan

Work Group Members
Lee Loong Koon, Tim Lim, Joseph Chiang, Chui Tau Siong, Jimmy Koh, Peter Law, Low Chow Hwee, K H Chan, Leslie Wong, Lawrence Mah, Wong Ngit Leong, Alfred Wong, T S Chew, Cheong Kok Hong, Jackson Koh, Danny Ng, C S Ang, Lee Siew Khuan, Joseph Putti, Sim Mong Chai, Wee Tiong Howe, T C Woo, Andrew Lee, Thio Gim Ho

SMEW *Work Group on Finance*
Steering Committee
Chairman: Peter Seah, Co-Chairman: Chua Soo Tian, Members: Lai Teck Poh, Lim Khian Geen, Ong Ai Boon, Wong See Meng, Teo Sok Nguang, Lim Tiong Wee, Ong Chye Lee, Leong Horn Kee, Foo Kok Swee, Su Kee Lay, Khor Seng Ping, Seet Quee Leong, Edwin Ong, Tan Jee Chin, Jahari bin Hj Affandi, Lim Chin Tong, Resource Organisations: Keith A K Tay, Victor Ng, Bernard Tay, Chia Li Leng, Chan Hwa Loon, Secretariat: Patrick Yang, Wynne Leong

Acknowledgements

Work Group Members

Samuel Lim, Boey Hong Khim, Kik Teng Guan, Lawrence Lee, Doreen Phua Wee Lim, James Chia, Bernard Chia, Chew Gian Sei, John Tan, Michael Koh, Pang Ee Ang, Paul Tan, Tan Boon Hock, Liong Thiam Keong, Michael Low, Toh Peng Kiat, Dennis Wong, James Chang, Tan Eng Joo, Gwee Yee Hean, Lee Hock Lai, Tay Kwang Seng, Lau Ee Hua, David Yeh

AGENDA FOR ACTION (1988)

Lee Hsien Loong, Abdullah Tarmugi, Eugene Yap, Othman Haron Eusofe, Tan Cheng Bock, Chng Hee Kok, Aline Wong, Ow Chin Hock, Lau Ping Sum

Resolutions Committee

Abdullah Tarmugi, David Tong, Wong Lam Wo, Kuan Kwee Jee, Cheng Huang Leng, Victor Ng, Tan Kim Hock, John Chen

Contributors

Lim Lay Ngoh, Tan Kee Soon, Chan Heng Wing, Matthias Yao, Lim Chin Siang, Abdul Halim Abdul Kader, Yusof Marican, Mok Song Ching, C F E Reincastle, Peh Chin Hua, PAP Party Branches: Boon Lay, Brickworks, Bukit Batok, Bukit Merah, Cairnhill, Delta, Jalan Besar, Jalan Kayu, Kg Glam, Kg Kembangan, Kolam Ayer, Leng Kee, Pasir Panjang, River Valley, Siglap, Tampines, Tanah Merah, Telok Blangah, Geylang West, Khe Bong, Teck Ghee, MacPherson, Tiong Bahru, Ang Mo Kio, Clementi, Fengshan, Geylang Serai, Jurong, Kebun Baru, Bedok, Bukit Panjang, Kallang, Toa Payoh, Yio Chu Kang, Alexander, Anson, Buona Vista, Cheng San, Chong Boon, Hong Kah, Joo Chiat, Kaki Bukit, Marine Parade, Nee Soon, West Coast, Ayer Rajah, Tanjong Pagar, Paya Lebar, Radin Mas, Braddell Heights, Tanglin, Changi, Chua Chu Kang, Kuo Chuan, Kim Seng, Kreta Ayer, Potong Pasir, Queenstown, Serangoon Gardens, Yuhua, Eunos, Henderson, Kg Ubi, Mountbatten, Moulmein, Sembawang, Telok Ayer

ECONOMIC COMMITTEE (1986)

Chairman: Lee Hsien Loong, Members: Nelson Britt, Koh Boon Hwee, Allan Ng Poh Meng, Tang I-Fang, Wan Soon Bee, Ang Kong Hua, Fock Siew Wah, Lim Kee Ming, Ngiam Tong Dow, Keith A K Tay, C N Watson

Sub-Committee on Manufacturing

Koh Boon Hwee, Ang Kong Hua, Nelson Britt, C N Watson, Cheng Wai Kueng, Jimmy Chew, Francis Siah, Tay Kwang Seng, Alan Yeo

Sub-Committee on Services

Tang I-Fang, Cham Tao Soon, Chan Sek Keong, Chang Kin Koon, Y C Chang, Goh Seng Kim, L J Holloway, Hong Hai, Robert Iau, Vince Khoo, Kwa Soon Bee, Lee Kum Tatt, Lee Ying Cheun, Stanley Liao, Sonnie Lien, Lim Hock San, Mah Bow Tan, Johnny Moo, Ngiam Tong Tau, Soong Chok Yean

Sub-Committee on Banking and Financial Services

Allan Ng Poh Meng, Fock Siew Wah, Ang Swee Tian, Chew Loy Kiat, Richard Crowder, Nicholas P Greville, Kwek Leng Beng, Lim Ho Kee, Kenneth G R MacLennan, Ng Kee Choe, Ong Tjin An, Peter Seah, Tjio Kay Loen

Sub-Committee on International Trade

S Chandra Das, Evert Henkes, John Huang, Koh Hock Seng, Leong Chee Whye, Francis Siah, Karmjit Singh, Bill Tan Tjo Tek, Tan Wah Thong, Wong Lin Hong

Sub-Committee on Local Businesses

Lim Kee Ming, Syed Ali Redha Alsagoff, Stephen Lee, Lim Hong Chee, Linn In Hua, G Ramachandran, Teo Soon Chuan, Whang Tar Liang

Sub-Committee on Entrepreneurship Development

Ang Kong Hua, Brian Chang, Eddie Foo, Goh Kian Chee, H H Haight, Ho Kwon Ping, Sia Yong, Tan Chin Tiong, Tan Wah Thong, S C Tien, Michael Yeo

Sub-Committee on Fiscal and Financial Policy

Keith A K Tay, David Blackett, Michael Brown, Hsieh Fu Hua, Sat Pal Khattar, Roger Lacey, Lo Hock Ling, Enrico Miserendino, Tan Chwee Huat, Teo Chiang Long, George Teo, Daniel Teo Tong How

Sub-Committee on Manpower

Wan Soon Bee, C N Watson, Hui Ban Yin, Lee Siong Kee, Ronald Lim Cheng Aun, Clement Ng, Ng Pock Too, Edward Tan

Secretariat

Patrick Daniel, Lau Kak En, Low Chin Nam, Tan Juinn Wen, Chan Kam Fai, Ho Cheok Kong, Long Chu, Evelyn Lim, Rhoda Lee, Connie Yee, Peggy Sim, Soh Wan Kuan, Khaw Sai Hoon, Lim Huey Chin, Tan Siew Pheng

MINISTRY OF EDUCATION PLANNING DIRECTORATE COMMITTEE (Ongoing)

Er Kwong Wah, John Yip Soon Kwong, Teo Hwee Choo, Pek Beng Choon, Lim Soon Tze, Wee Heng Tin, Tan See Lai, Kam Kum Wone, Ang Wai Hoong

PRIMARY EDUCATION COMMITTEE (Ongoing)

Seet Ai Mee, Sidek Saniff, Tang Guan Seng, Er Kwong Wah, John Yip Soon Kwong, Wee Heng Tin, Lim Soon Tze, Ang Wai Hoong, Kan Sou Tin, Charlotte Beck, Seah Jiak Choo

ECONOMIC PLANNING COMMITTEE (Ongoing)

Chairman: Mah Bow Tan, Members: Lam Chuan Leong, Philip Yeo, Yeo Seng Teck, Tan Chin Nam, Quek Poh Huat, Cham Tao Soon, Koh Beng Seng, Robert Chua, Leong Chee Whye, Lim Ho Kee, Rafiq Jumabhoy, Cheng Hong Kok, Resource Persons: Lim Chin, Peter Connell, Tan Kong Yam, Linda Low, Toh Mun Heng, Wong Seng Hon, Secretariat: Daniel Selvaretnam, Francis Yuen, Balagopal Nair, Sonny Tan

Contributors

Goh Keng Swee, George Yeo, Augustine H H Tan, Albert Winsemius, Pieter Winsemius

Manufacturing Sub-Committee

Chairman: Philip Yeo, Members: Lam Chuan Leong, Cham Tao Soon, Koh Juan Kiat, Liew Mun Leong, Robert Chua, Lim Ho Kee, Resource Persons: Lim Chin, Peter Connell

Services Sub-Committee

Chairman: Yeo Seng Teck, Members: Koh Beng Seng, Lim Swee Say, How Peck Huat, Rafiq Jumabhoy, Tang Wee Sung, Lim Koon Sang, Resource Persons: Ko Kheng Hwa, Linda Low

Acknowledgements

Secretariat for Manufacturing and Services Sub-Committees
Lee Suan Hiang, Sonny Tan, Tam-Lai Seow Yoke, Linda Sein, Ngiam Ai Choo, Helen Luk, Aleth Wee, Nancy Wang, Soh Szu Wei, Evelyn Chen, Darshan Singh

Future Vision Sub-Committee
Chairman: Tan Chin Nam, Members: Ng Kiat Chong, Pek Hock Thiam, Leong Chee Whye, Patrick Daniel, Ho Kwon Ping, Resource Persons: Tan Kong Yam, Lim Swee Say, Wong Seng Hon, Ko Kheng Hwa, Secretariat: Balagopal Nair, Judy Tan, Yong Yaw Nam

Environment Scan Sub-Committee
Chairman: Quek Poh Huat, Members: Lim Hock San, Sung Sio Ma, Ho Tian Yee, Cheng Hong Kok, Resource Persons: Toh Mun Heng, Wong Seng Hon, Secretariat: Francis Yuen, Chang Siew Ngoh, Chan Keng Luck, Leroy Lim

Task Forces
Chairmen: Lim Hock San, Cheng Hong Kok, Sung Sio Ma, Ho Tian Yee, Quek Poh Huat, Members: Eddie Teo, Low Choon Ming, Tan Yong Soon, Leslie Fong, Derek Da Cunha, Chin Kin Wah, Ho Cheok Sun, Bhanoji Rao, Donald V Grant, Charles Pope, Low Sin Leng, Tien Sing Cheong, Lee Suan Hiang, Gong Wee Lik, Ng Kim Neo, Johnny Lim, Robin Tan, Lim Soon Hock, Sin Hang Boon, Ho Lam Phoh, Jeff Mowla, Lim Chuan Poh, Cheng Wai Keung, Yvon Mace, Diana Tsaw, Liew Mun Leong, Cham Tao Soon, Poo Aun Neow, Ho Ching, Joseph Chen, Chris Yong, Francis Yuen, Secretariat: Ng Ee Peng, Fred Gan, Ow Peng Seang, Chan Keng Luck, Chen Fui Lin

LOCAL ENTERPRISE COORDINATING COMMITTEE (Ongoing)
Chairman: Philip Yeo, Members: Pek Hock Thiam, Koh Juan Kiat, Lim Swee Say, Lai Seck Khui, Liew Mun Leong, Tan Chin Nam, Yeo Seng Teck

INSTITUTE OF MANUFACTURING TECHNOLOGY ADVISORY COMMITTEE (Ongoing)
Chairman: Leong Cheng Chit, Members: Chan Hua Bee, Choo Chiau Beng, Gan Kim Song, Goh Chin Khee, Henry Y Hayashi, Khoo Lee Meng, Robert Kirchgaessner, Chris Koh, Patrick Lian, Leslie Lim, James Ling, Christer Ronnegard, M Sekiya, James Teo, Wee Yue Chew, Yap Kian Tiong, Secretariat: James Ng

SERVICES SECTOR POLICY COMMITTEE (Ongoing)
Chairman: Philip Yeo, Members: Kwa Soon Bee, Er Kwong Wah, Tan Guong Ching, Goh Kim Leong, Tan Chin Tiong, Koh Cher Siang, Yeo Seng Teck, Lim Swee Say, Wong Hung Khim, Ngiam Tong Tau, Pek Hock Thiam, Lim Hock San, Quek Poh Huat, Lam Siew Wah, Ng Kiat Chong, Koh Beng Seng, Pek Siok Ching, S Tiwari, Liu Thai Ker, Tan Chin Nam, How Peck Huat

NATIONAL BIOTECHNOLOGY COMMITTEE (Ongoing)
Chairman: Y H Tan, Members: Chan Soh Ha, Chua Nam Hai, Louis Lim, Ngiam Tong Tau, Teoh Yong Sea, Peter Yeo

SMALL AND MEDIUM ENTERPRISE RETAIL PLAN (SMERP) CONSULTATIVE COMMITTEE (Ongoing)
Chairman: Philip Yeo, Members: Tan Chin Nam, Chuang Kwong Yong, Khoo Teng Chye, Lim Swee Say, Koh Juan Kiat, Pek Hock Thiam, Lai Seck Khui, Ernest Wong, Tan Eng Joo, Jalil Haron, T R Mulani, Steven Goh, Tan Chong Meng

SMERP Work Group on Retail Infrastructure
Co-Chairmen: Au Eng Kok, Chuang Kwong Yong, Members: William Seet, Larry Chua, Koh Seow Chuan, Yang Ai Fong, Fong Chun Wah, Goh-Sim Teow Leng, Wong Kok Seng, Teh Ban Lian, Lawrence Hair, Ong Chang Sam, Chionh Chye Khye, Loh Ah Tuan, Resource Organisation: Corinne Yap, Ruyee How

SMERP Work Group on Retail Efficiency
Chairmen: Tang Wee Sung, Foo Meng Tong, Members: Andrew Lim, Jannie Tay, Lim Yue Khim, Robert Iau, A P Subhash C Metha, R S Wickramasuriya, Dee Richmond, Arthur Lee, Lim Choon, Goh Suay Tee, Soh Yoke Chai, Mohd Salleh, Lynn Ho-Tan, Resource Organisation: Steven Lim

SMERP Project Work Group
Chairmen: Gan Eng Oon, Tony Tan Keng Joo, Members: Davinder Singh, Edward Wong, Kwek Theng Swee, William S W Lim, Lim Woon Kiat, Peter Lai, Foo Meng Tong, Lee Loong Koon, Resource Organisation: Wang Look Tsui

SMERP Work Group on Distribution
Chairmen: Lim Ho Seng, Lim Swee Say, Alt Co-Chairman: Ko Kheng Hwa, Members: Bill Liu, Tan Jin Soon, K P Wun, Lim Lee Chong, Pearleen Chan, William Choo, Tan Kay Hock, Chew Tuan Gee, Amit Banerji, Goo Kem Suaa, Ling Kong Beng, Goh Chin Siew, Liao Chung Lik, Chor Nguk Yuen, Resource Organisation: Quek Soo Tat

SMERP Work Group on Human Resource Management
Chairmen: Steven Goh, Koh Juan Kiat, Alt Chairmen: Victor Tan, Chew Whye, Members: Foo Der Rong, Joseph Tan, Lim Woon Kiat, Ashok B Melwani, Franciscus Tan, Wang Ting-Min, Tan Teck Meng, Lee Loong Koon, Elaine Ang, Ng Ah Seng, Ho Chan Sian, Kwek Theng Swee, Chua Song Peck, Foo Tai Kin, Gan Chee Toh, Resource Organisation: Hamish Christie, Lim Chiang

LEISURE INDUSTRY DEVELOPMENT (Ongoing)
Lifestyle 2000 Committee
Chairman: Liu Thai Ker, Members: Lam Chuan Leong, Lim Leong Geok, Leong Chee Whye, Tan Chin Nam, Yeo Seng Teck, Pek Hock Thiam, Lai Seck Khui, Goh Hup Chor, How Peck Huat, Steven Yeo

159

Picture Credits

Munshi Ahmed, Chua Soo Bin,
Rio Helmi, Tommy Koh, Leong Ka Tai,
Albert Lim, Lawrence Lim, Tuck Loong,
Pan Shou, KF Seetoh, Russell Wong.

Anderson Junior College, Bedok South
Secondary School, Curriculum Development
Institute of Singapore, Economic
Development Board, Housing Development
Board, Institute of Education, Institute of
Molecular and Cell Biology, Ministry of
Communications and Information,
Ministry of Community Development,
Ministry of Defence, Ministry of Education,
Ministry of Foreign Affairs, Ministry of
Health, Ministry of National Development,
Nanyang Junior College, Nanyang
Technological Institute, National
Productivity Board, National University of
Singapore, People's Association, Peranakan
Place, Pioneer Magazine, Port of Singapore
Authority, Siglap Secondary School,
Singapore Airlines Ltd, Singapore Armed
Forces, Singapore Council of Social Service,
Singapore Dance Theatre, Singapore Labour
Foundation, Singapore Mass Rapid Transit
Corporation, Singapore Polytechnic,
Singapore Sports Council, Singapore Tourist
Promotion Board, Tao Nan Primary School,
The Salvation Army, Urban Redevelopment
Authority, Victoria Junior College,
Vocational and Industrial Training Board,
Wearne Brothers Services (Pte) Ltd.

Editorial and Design team

Shirley Hew, Shova Loh, Tuck Loong,
Edmund Lam, Goh Sui Noi, Jamilah Mohd Hassan,
Leonard Lau, Roseline Lum, Siow Peng Han,
Tan Kok Eng, Lee Woon Hong, Ong Su Ping,
Katherine Tan, Ang Siew Lian, Thomas Koh.